Beware
the
New
Prophets

An Updated Caution of
the Modern Prophetic Movement

including an analysis of
Mike Bickle, Bill Johnson, and Todd Bentley

Bill Randles

BEWARE THE NEW PROPHETS:
An Updated Caution of the Modern Prophetic Movement
including an analysis of Mike Bickle, Bill Johnson, and Todd Bentley

Copyright © 2015 Bill Randles
Second edition: revised and updated
First edition Copyright © 1999 Bill Randles

Published by:
Believers in Grace Ministries
8585 C Avenue
Marion, Iowa 52302

ISBN: 978-0-6925332-0-8

For more information about the author or his ministry, contact
Billlrandles.Wordpress.com or believersingrace.com.

Except where otherwise indicated, all Scripture quotations in this book are taken from the King James Version of the Bible.

PRINTED IN THE UNITED STATES OF AMERICA

Dedication

To my longsuffering and loving wife, Kristin Randles. You have stood with me in the good fight of faith. Truly we are a team for Jesus, and I thank God for you.

Also to my home church, Believers in Grace Fellowship in Cedar Rapids, Iowa. You have stood fast in the battle and have supported this and many other good works. I thank the Lord for these faithful people in my life. May God bless them all.

Contents

By Jacob Prasch

WHEN THE LORD JESUS, the apostles, and the Hebrew prophets repeatedly warned of the emergence of false prophets in the last days, most Christians have taken that to mean to non-Christian and pseudo-Christian cults outside of the Body of Christ. To most of us it means the Mormons, the Jehovah's Witnesses, the Unification Church, Christian Scientists or some other clearly heretical group. Often, traditional Calvinistic Christians influenced by the historicist eschatology of Reformed theology have applied these warnings to the Roman Catholic, Eastern Orthodox or liberal Protestant churches, but not to evangelicals.

A closer reading of the warnings of Jesus and the apostles however make it clear that these false prophets would come among true believers with a mandate from hell to deceive the very elect, in the same way as Israel's false prophets misled Israel (Matthew 7:15, Matthew 24:24, Acts 20:30).

I have been in no doubt that the proliferation of wild deceptions in the church in recent years is being propagated by those very men Paul warned would come in the last times "going from bad to worse, deceiving and being deceived" (2 Timothy 3:13). Neither do I doubt that these trends are preludes to the great *apostasia* or falling away we are told to expect (2 Thessalonians 2:3), paving the way for the ultimate ascendancy of the Man of Lawlessness.

Central to this deception has been a near endless stream of men and women claiming a prophetic office, complete with predictive prophesy, but ignoring that the failure of these predictions made in the Lord's name is the biblical proof demonstrating them to be false prophets (Deuteronomy 18:20-22). This trend is presently going from bad to worse, and before the Return of Jesus will become worse still. The Restoration Movement, Kingdom Now Reconstructionists, most of the popular Charismatic Movement, and now much of not only Pentecostalism, but even non-Charismatics influenced by reconstructionism are being more and more given to heeding the voices of those proven to prophesy falsely.

The Word of the Lord assures us that when these deceptions come, men who understand will take action and give understanding to the many as the Maccabees did in the days of Antiochus Epiphanes (Daniel 11:33-35).

As is evidenced by his previous two books, I believe my dear friend and brother Bill Randles has been shown by the Lord to be one of those who know their God and take such action. Bill is a pastor with a shepherd's heart for the Lord's sheep. His motive in writing this book has not been unholy anger, pride, self aggrandizement, or jealousy. His motive has been to help protect the Lord's flock, to make other pastors aware of what is going on and to provide them with the material they need to withstand the deceptions that destroy and the wolves that devour.

The church, like Israel, has always had false prophets, but not since the early church have we witnessed as many nor as diverse an array of them as we see today paraded before us one after another on what represents itself to be Christian TV. While the times are treacherous we can rejoice that Jesus is indeed coming soon. One sign of this is the incredible multiplication of these false prophets deceiving the elect. Another sign of His return however is the rise of those who repel the onslaught at our very gate (Isaiah 28:6).

In view of the urgency of the hour I commend this book to you, that you in turn will be like the Bereans who "examin[ed] the Scriptures daily to see whether these things were so." (Acts 17:11 NASB)

"An appalling and horrible thing
Has happened in the land:
The prophets prophesy falsely,
And the priests rule on their own authority;
And My people love it so!
But what will you do at the end of it?
(Jeremiah 5:30–31 NASB)

What Will You Do in the End?

A wonderful and horrible thing is committed in the land;
The prophets prophesy falsely, and the priests bear rule
by their means; and my people love to have it so: and
what will ye do in the end thereof? (Jeremiah 5:30-31)

THE PROPHET JEREMIAH ASKED a very important question of those among God's people who had so readily rushed after the many false prophets of his own day. A paraphrase of the question would sound somewhat like this, "Where are these false prophets taking you? What will be the end of their fake 'words' and glib assurances?" In the case of Judah, the end was very grim indeed.

The people of Judah much preferred the plethora of false prophecies over the sober warning and pleading of Jeremiah to submit to Babylon as a tool of God's discipline .

"Words" were circulated all the way up to the king himself, assuring the speedy restoration of Judah to greatness, the recovery of the royal family which had been taken away into exile by Nebuchadnessar, and the breaking off of the yoke of the Babylonians.

Appealing catchphrases gave false assurance to the backslidden congregation of the Lord, such as the phrase, "The Temple of the LORD, The Temple of the LORD . . .," as though Jerusalem was inviolable because of the presence of the temple.

Such is the power of delusion. The human heart tends to deceive itself and to willingly be deceived, as Jeremiah reminds us:

The heart is deceitful above all things, and desperately wicked: who can know it? I the Lord search the heart, I try the reins, even to give every man according to his ways, and according to the fruit of his doings. (Jeremiah 17:9-10)

The end came as a terror.

After a nightmare siege, the walls of Jerusalem were breached, the Temple of God was destroyed, tens of thousands of Jews were slaughtered in the streets, and thousands more of them were tied together and marched off into captivity 400 miles away, never to be seen again, for the most part, until a small remnant of them returned 70 years later.

They should have listened to Jeremiah. They could have been spared, the temple and city might have also been preserved.

But for every Jeremiah, there are always a couple of dozen Hannaniahs.

> And it came to pass the same year, in the beginning of the reign of Zedekiah king of Judah, in the fourth year, and in the fifth month, that Hananiah the son of Azur the prophet, which was of Gibeon, spake unto me in the house of the Lord, in the presence of the priests and of all the people, saying, Thus speaketh the Lord of hosts, the God of Israel, saying, I have broken the yoke of the king of Babylon.

> Within two full years will I bring again into this place all the vessels of the Lord's house, that Nebuchadnezzar king of Babylon took away from this place, and carried them to Babylon: And I will bring again to this place Jeconiah the son of Jehoiakim king of Judah, with all the captives of Judah, that went into Babylon, saith the Lord: for I will break the yoke of the king of Babylon. Then the prophet Jeremiah said unto the prophet Hananiah in the presence of the priests, and in the presence of all the people that stood in the house of the

Lord . . . Amen: the Lord do so: the Lord perform thy words which thou hast prophesied, to bring again the vessels of the Lord's house, and all that is carried away captive, from Babylon into this place.

Nevertheless hear thou now this word that I speak in thine ears, and in the ears of all the people; The prophets that have been before me and before thee of old prophesied both against many countries, and against great kingdoms, of war, and of evil, and of pestilence. The prophet which prophesieth of peace, when the word of the prophet shall come to pass, then shall the prophet be known, that the Lord hath truly sent him . . . **Then said the prophet Jeremiah unto Hananiah the prophet, Hear now, Hananiah; The Lord hath not sent thee; but thou makest this people to trust in a lie.** (Jeremiah 28:1-8,15, emphasis added)

Now we find ourselves in a very similar situation to that of Jeremiah and Judah.

We too are on the verge of the final Judgment and time of testing of the whole earth. Judgment begins in the house of God. At a time when Christians ought to be readying themselves, alert and aware of what is going on, as the apostles admonished us to be, the church is in the midst of a wave of false prophets and apostles, deceiving people with false "words" from God, and leading them into Gnosticism, mysticism and even the occult.

For more than twenty years, many have sought to sound the alarm, and to warn the church of these false prophets, as Jeremiah did in his day. Wonderful men of God such as Chuck Smith, David Wilkerson, Dave Hunt, Jacob Prasch, and many others have written books and personally cried out against the charlatons and fakes such as the Kansas City Prophets, John Wimber, Kenneth Copeland, Benny Hinn, Rodney Howard Browne and Todd Bentley.

But the "Prophetic" movement proceeds anyway, corrupting the church, destroying lives by issuing false "words," ludicrous visions and dreams, teaching false and even dangerous doctrines, promoting fake "revivals," exploiting the gullible and perhaps worst of all, leading the young and untaught, like the Pied Piper, out of the churches and into the New Age movement.

It is now 17 years since I wrote this book, *Beware the New Prophets*. We have had time to consider the answer to the question Jeremiah asked in the opening scripture. Where has the Prophetic movement taken the church? Have the "great swelling words" of prophecy been fulfilled? Has the church entered into the age of revival and power evangelism that the prophets proclaimed?

By now many of the "prophets" we warned of, have died. John Wimber, Paul Cain and Bob Jones have all passed away. Cain and Jones, once regarded by the leaders of the movement as "The great power of God"(Like Simon Magus in Acts 8), and as "The terror of the Lord," both died in disgrace, having separately been exposed as sexual deviants.

John Paul Jackson now teaches "dream interpretation," as his "Stream Ministries" website advertises.

> Dream Expert, John Paul Jackson, decodes the meaning of dreams in new Fall show, Dreams and Mysteries. Effective dream interpretation can provide answers, insights, ideas and spiritual guidance.

> Dreams and their meaning shaped the government, religion and daily life of ancient cultures. Most ancient cultures believed that dreams were either direct messages or were symbols requiring interpretation of the mysterious code. Dream journals have been found in Mesopotamia and Egypt. Today, the mystery of dreams are explored by psychiatrists and exploited by Hollywood box office hits. To help people decode the meaning of their dreams, dream expert John Paul Jackson

is hosting a new show Dreams and Mysteries, premiering this October.

"Dreams speak in a code or symbolic language that uses objects, activities, places and people to instruct us," explains John Paul Jackson, Dream Expert and Founder of Streams Ministries. "The impact of a dream is only as good as the interpretation. To have a correct interpretation one has to know the dream source and dream code."[1]

Mike Bickle still maintains that the Kansas City Prophets were valid and are foundational to his IHOP (International House Of Prayer) ministry. Thousands of young people pour into the retreats at IHOP centers, to be inducted into contemplative prayer, the teachings of the Roman Catholic mystics, and to be brought into an ecstatic "worship style" which borders on the erotic, in their pursuit of "Passion for Jesus."

Rodney Howard Browne is still holding "revivals" featuring irrational laughter, trances, spiritual drunkenness and experienced-based Christianity. He has never renounced the "God's Bartender" teachings that brought hundreds of thousands into an irrational form of "worship."

There are others who have taken the mantle from the early pioneers of this heretical and dangerous movement and gone further. Not further into the Spirit of the LORD but further into the occult.

Ekstasis: a New Level of "Worship"

HAVE YOU HEARD OF the new level of worship called Ekstasis? It is heavily promoted by Patricia King, a "prophetic leader" who is the host of a television show called Extreme Prophetic Evangelism.

Patricia King was an early promoter of the heavily tattooed, and violent healing evangelist, Todd Bentley, who was featured on the show as one of the new prophets of the younger generation. Patricia King spoke for many when she proclaimed Todd as an "awesome man of power who is a Seer." She also announced that Todd has brought "a million people into the Kingdom of God in the last eight years."

Todd was guest on the show with his mentor, another "great "prophet"—Bob Jones. His resume was equally impressive. King described him as "a champion of the Seer realm," and "one of the most accurate of prophets of our generation." Bentley himself has great reverence for Bob Jones. When Bentley prepares for his yearly visitation of the Lord, to seek what is the word for the year to come, part of the preparation involves consulting with Jones. He says,

> . . . needing a clear commission from the Lord concerning direction for the year, I always seek him about what lies ahead. With that purpose, recently, I asked my friend Bob Jones (a gifted, mature seer-prophet) about what God was saying to him concerning 2008 . . .[2]

On the same television show, King introduced the world to Caleb Brundage and his "Club Mysterio." Brundage is a DJ and worship leader at the club, which features regular gatherings of young "worshipers," who openly seek to enter into ecstatic trances through repetitive beats of electronic worship songs.

Caleb Brundage describes Ekstasis on the Elijah List website:

> The Lord has revealed that many in this hour who will worship Him will actually be taken into His ecstasy. These ones will find themselves lost in His wonderment, amazed by Him and His miracles, going into places in worship they have never been before. Due to their newly found freedom in Jesus, some of these individuals will be freed from the prison of their souls as they experience this new level of worship - Ekstasis Worship.[3]

Brundage goes on to define Ekstasis as being, "freedom from the confines of time and space," a "trance," "throwing of the mind out of a normal state," and even "insane"! Brundage points out that the word for trance in Acts 11:5 is "Ekstasis," and then equates the trance state with "being in the presence of God"

> Here the word trance is also ekstasis in the Greek. We see ekstasis being used in the definition of moving beyond oneself. Here is, I believe, a state of being in the presence of God. I see this happening as people are praising God in the dance. Psalm 150 says to praise Him in the dance. The psalms say He inhabits the praises of His people. The sheet comes down and He comes and sits in your praise dance.[4]

WHERE HAS THIS MISGUIDED movement taken us? What will become of the young people, who have been deceived into accepting the pagan idea that irrationality and ecstasy are the route to an un-mediated experience of God?

Why would any of these young people want to seriously study Scripture and patiently pray to God, with no feeling at all, developing the virtues of endurance and patience, when instead they can go to an Ekstasis rave?

The idea that one day, evangelical Christian youth would flock to "clubs" that they might knowingly be swayed by an endless repetitive synthesized beat, until they are induced into an ecstatic "Trance State," and to call it "worship" and "the presence of God," would have been unthinkable to those of us born again in the late 1970s and early '80s.

True worship and the knowledge of God have been redefined by the Prophetic movement, and the mystical "Toronto/Pensacola (false) revival" from which it emerged.

Definitely one of the places where the false prophets have brought many to, is experience-based spirituality.

I hope to show by the additions to this book, that "the end" of following these prophets, is not a blissful experience of God as promised, but rather a delusion, a hollowing out of faith, and even a slide into the occult.

1

The Explosion of New Prophets

> I am sending a whole generation of prophets to you. I
> am about to release prophecy on the church as you have
> never seen it before . . . I have a secret plan, and that
> plan is being unfolded here a little, there a little. Listen
> to the prophets—the little prophets, the big prophets,
> listen to those who speak one line and to those who
> speak volumes . . . false religion will literally dry up in
> your day. False religion will go off radio and television. It
> will lack the funds to continue.[1] —Pastor Glenn Foster

OVER THE LAST FEW decades, the Christian church has been in-
undated with self-proclaiming prophets and apostles—they call
themselves "the new prophets." With their bold personas and even
bolder utterances, they have captured the imagination of millions
of Christians who have become discontented with simple faith
in the Scriptures and have hungered for "more." From where do
these prophets come? What theological justification do they give
for their claims? Most importantly, how do we judge whether they
are of God or not? These are some of the questions I know many
are asking. In this book, I shall let these prophets and apostles
speak for themselves so you can be the judge of what these men
and women really believe. If these prophets are from God, we need
them, but if they are false prophets, they pose a great threat to the
purity, credibility, and integrity of the church. If false, they are
especially dangerous to those who are young in the faith. Let's take

a look at these new prophets, their prophecies, and their teachings.

This advertisement in *Charisma Magazine* caught my eye. It was announcing an upcoming "Seers Convocation":

> INTERNATIONAL SEERS CONVOCATION
> EAST MEETS WEST
> AND SUNRISE MEETS SUNSET
> PROPHET E. BERNARD JORDAN
> AND PROPHET VERNON ASHE
> COMING TOGETHER
> TO UNVEIL ANCIENT TRUTHS
> FOR THE NEW MILLENNIUM,
> TRUTHS THAT WILL HELPYOU
> UNLOCK YOUR PROPHETIC ABILITY . . .

This full page advertisement in *Charisma* went on to inform readers that:

> Prophet Jordan has summoned his newly formed company of prophets to minister to you prophetically. When you register, you'll get your personal appointment with the prophets and a free copy of Bishop Jordan's book, *Seeds of Destiny* . . . Before you make another decision in life, let the prophets help you unlock your gift of prophecy.[2]

It should be noted that in Amos 7:12, the word "seer" is used derisively, as of someone who has hallucinations and should not to be taken seriously!

Jordan is far from unique. There are scores of prophets these days, from the rapping South African Kim Clement to Rick Joyner and his visions of talking eagles, angelic guided tours of paradise, and conversations with the enthroned departed saints. There is a wide range of the "prophetic," and it is being taken quite seriously by many within the evangelical/Protestant world. When Christians participate in events such as March for Jesus and Promise Keepers, they are unwittingly involving themselves in this "prophetic" ministry.

A trip through almost any Christian bookstore would confirm that indeed we are in the midst of a "great" prophetic movement and that it has been steadily increasing for the last thirty years. Titles such as *Prophets and Personal Prophecy*; *The Prophetic Ministry; Apostles, Prophets and the Coming Move of God*; *Adventures in the Prophetic*; and *Growing in the Prophetic* are among the dozens, even hundreds, of titles that have poured out of the Christian presses offering help in dream interpretation, how to develop your prophetic gifting, how to become receptive to the ministry of prophets, even how to compose prophetic songs!

The new prophets (and prophetesses) are no longer restricted to the margins of popular Christian experience either; they are in infuential positions. James Ryle, for example, was the pastor of the thriving Boulder Colorado Vineyard (now called Vinelife Church) for over fifteen years, and today considers himself a modern-day prophet. Ryle was also involved heavily with Promise Keepers and mentored PK's founder Bill McCartney. Promise Keepers is seen by many as the fulfillment of the prophecies of Paul Cain and Bob Jones, two "prophets" whom you will meet later. Ryle's book, *Hippo in the Garden*, was based on a dream he had, which the title describes. One of Ryle's specialties has been dream interpretation, and the interpretation of the hippo dream was that there would shortly be coming to the church a prophetic movement which would seem as out of place as a hippo in a garden!

Paul Cain, another of the more prominent prophets, is supposed to have gone to President George Bush with a prophecy while Bush was in office, and other world leaders have recognized his prophetic gifting, including Saddam Hussein (Yes, THAT Saddam!). Rodney Howard Browne, Bill Hamon, Rick Joyner,

Kenneth Copeland and others who claim to be prophets, have consistently prophesied that the new prophets would be consulted by world leaders, kings, and heads of nations.

The prophetic movement offers a whole worldview. One discernment ministry explains:

> When the New Apostolic Reformation (NAR) talks about re-aligning the Church to the supposed 5-fold ministry structure of Ephesians 4:11, the new doctrinal emphasis is placed on laying a "foundation" of prophets and apostles. These "offices" are looked upon as key for future church governance. These new prophets are claimed to possess authority to bring unity, knowledge, maturity, collaboration and growth.[3]

To the prophets, the eighties was the prophetic decade, and the nineties was the decade designated as the time for the restoration of the apostles, who are to bring in a "special governmental anointing" which will radically reform the church. Some of these modern prophets say that Christianity will be entirely (redeemed?) by these apostles. In Bill Hamon's book, *Prophets and Personal Prophecy*, Hamon states:

> Christ cannot return until His ascension gift ministries have brought the church into full manhood. The Pastor, Evangelist and Teacher have been the only ones acknowledged as being active in that role. But now, Christ is activating His Prophets in the 1980s and His Apostles in the 1990s. Jesus is thrilled at the thought that His prophets will soon be fully recognized by the church.[4]

This new breed of prophets is not in any way cautious about taking to themselves the title of "prophet" or calling themselves "anointed." They see themselves as specially chosen by God to lead and prophesize the church. They tell Christian believers that the church needs them to know God's will and have His guidance. But is such an anointing only for a chosen few? Theologian Dr. Harry Ironside doesn't think so. In referencing 1 John 2: 12-29, he states:

> It is to the babes he says, in verse 20, "Ye have an unction [or, anointing] from the Holy One, and ye know all things." And again, in verse 27, while still addressing the youngest and feeblest of saints he writes, "But the anointing which ye have received of Him abideth in you, and ye need not that any man teach you, but as the same anointing teacheth you of all things , and is truth, and is no lie, and even as it hath taught you, ye shall abide in Him." The anointing then is the portion of the babe in Christ; how much more of the young men and fathers. All Christians are anointed. In fact, this is involved in the very name divinely given them. Christ means the "anointed." Christians are anointed ones, by the Spirit linked with their glorified Head. By the anointing our understanding is opened that we may understand the Scriptures and be kept from Satanic perversions of the truth.[5]

As believers, we need to be Bereans and to discern and test all things as Scripture tells us to do. The Bereans were considered noble because they were not blindly accepting what the Apostle Paul said, but sought the Scriptures to see "whether those things were so." (Acts 17:11)

It is this kind of thinking that is being strangled to death as often as possible by the new, bold, manipulative "prophets" and "apostles" whose constant mantra is something to the effect that "God is so much bigger than His Word" or "God is offending our minds so that He can reach our hearts," and of course one of the more manipulative, "Most Christians have more faith in Satan's ability to deceive us than in God's ability to bless us." This is starkly contrasted to God's own perspective which is expressed by David, who praises God for the fact that ". . . thou hast magnified thy word above all thy name." (Psalm 138:2)

The effect of this steady drumbeat has been to disarm the believer of his ability to make the critical judgments needed to "Be sober, be vigilant, because your adversary the devil, as a roaring lion, walketh about, seeking whom he may devour." (1 Peter 5:8)

At a time when sobriety is desperately needed, spiritual drunkenness is being promoted to the unwary, and people are being seduced by the idea that as the great Last Days overcomers, ("cutting edge Christians," the "manchild company") discernment is the last thing with which they need to be concerned. Perhaps we can yet rouse some to "Buy the truth, and sell it not" (Proverbs 23:23), and awaken others out of their drunken slumber, "redeeming the time, because the days are evil" (Ephesians 5:16).

2

The Theology
of the New Prophets

God's people are going to start to exercise rule, and
they're going to take dominion over the power of Satan.
They're going to bring diabolical princes down. The
dark powers that hover over the parliament buildings of
the nations are going to be paralyzed by the corporate
prayer of an authoritative community. As the rod of His
strength goes out of Zion, He'll change legislation. He'll
chase the devil off the face of God's earth, and God's
people together, doing the will of God, will bring about
God's purposes and God's reign.[1] —Ern Baxter

THE ONLY WAY TO understand the teachings and utterances of the
new prophets is to look at the underlying theological framework
that has informed most of them. The prophetic movement has
come out of the Pentecostal world and, particularly, the late 1940s
revival called the New Order of the Latter Rain. From the Latter
Rain movement came the Manifested Sons of God heresy, which
was renounced by the Assemblies of God in 1949. Though it was
discredited, its ideals have taken on a heretical life of their own.
They have resurfaced under a different name and have been promoted by various personalities.

At the turn of the last century, the Pentecostal revival exploded
on the world scene. People from all walks of life were touched by

the revival. After Word War II, a virtual explosion of Pentecostal evangelists came on the scene, and before long, names such as A. A. Allen, T. L. Osborn, Oral Roberts, and Jack Coe became household words. These evangelists emphasized salvation and divine healing, and were very innovative in the use of the media. Radio and eventually television became the means of expansion to many Pentecostal ministries, and gradually the expectation began to change for many Pentecostals. The old line Pentecostals had a simple message, for the most part, "Jesus saves, Jesus heals, Jesus baptizes in the Holy Spirit, and Jesus is coming again."(Again, we need to be careful. Osborn, Roberts, Coe all stressed false teachings as well as the salvation message.) They also stressed the "power of the blood" of Jesus and the hope of Jesus' soon return. It permeates the hymnody—for example, songs like "I'll Fly Away," "Changed in the Twinkling of an Eye," "We Shall See the King," and so forth. The early Pentecostals held no stock in this world. They longed for the dawning of the coming new day, inaugurated at the coming of the Lord Jesus. Unlike their current pneumo-centric (spirit centered) offspring, the early Pentecostals were passionately Christocentric! (We need to define "early Pentecostals." T. L. Osborn, Jack Coe, and Oral Roberts all fostered tremendous heresy.) But with the new found success and the seeming power of the new evangelists, preachers and teachers began to talk about the "new thing" that God was going to be doing.

What do we mean, "new thing?" It comes from Isaiah 43:19, "Behold I do a new thing; now it shall spring forth; shall ye not know it?" According to the principles of hermeneutics (biblical interpretation), the new thing which God promised to Israel is contrasted to the old thing which they had already been experiencing. But, according to the new teachers, the new thing is still to come, a "Great Last Days Revival," that will supposedly sweep in the world for Jesus, bringing whole nations into the Kingdom. Thus gradually, instead of looking for the bodily return of Jesus, the focus was switched to the day when we would come into our own great power and glory—the "new thing." This explains why Christians who have been saved by Jesus and filled with the Holy Spirit are willing to jump on planes, charter buses, and travel great distances upon the report of a possible outbreak of the "new thing." Neither is this a recent phenomenon. It goes back further than Toronto and Pensacola. People have been seeking this "new thing" for at least fifty years!

Another similarly misinterpreted scriptural concept is the Latter Rain. Hosea 6:3, Joel 2:23, and James 5:7 speak of the latter rain. Once again, hermeneutics comes into play. The terms "former and latter rain" refer allegorically to the agricultural calendar of the land of Israel. The former rain, which was vital to the preparation of the soil for planting season, corresponds to the law of Moses. It does to people's hearts what the plowing does to the ground, such as breaking up the hardness and convicting of sin. "The law of the Lord is perfect, converting the soul" (Psalm 19:7). The latter rains in Israel are essential for the perfecting of the crop for harvest. This corresponds to the giving of the Spirit on Pentecost.

It is the Spirit who prepares hearts to be harvested for Jesus, and who gives life. Interestingly enough, both the giving of the law and the sending of the Spirit took place on the Feast of Pentecost. The number 3000 is also involved in both of these, for after the giving of the law, Israel rebelled and 3000 were slain. After the giving of the Spirit, Peter preached and 3000 were saved. ". . . for the letter killeth, but the Spirit giveth life" (2 Corinthians 3:6). But, like the new thing, the Latter Rain concept evolved into an expectation of something other than the indwelling of the Spirit—a coming "outpouring." The Former Rain was now interpreted as Pentecost, or even Azusa Street, but something even greater was about to break forth. Rather than proclaiming the hoped for *Parousia*, the bodily return of Jesus, the preaching and prophecies began to focus on the things we would be doing in the "next great revival." The actual coming of Jesus as an imminent reality was actually taught by some to be an impossibility, on the grounds that the church had not yet restored "all things."

Where did they get this idea? From another badly distorted Scripture, Acts 3:20-21:

> And he shall send Jesus Christ, which before was preached unto you: whom the heaven must receive until the time of restitution of all things, which God hath spoken by the mouth of all His holy prophets since the world began.

The context for this Scripture, hermeneutically, is the Temple, addressed to the Jews, who were awaiting their Messiah, the one whom they believed would restore the Davidic fortunes of Israel. Peter points to the restoration of the cripple in the name of Jesus, and proclaims that it attests to the fact that the Messiah they awaited was the one that they failed to recognize and had crucified and slain. This one whom they had rejected, God has vindicated by the resurrection of Jesus, and upon Israel's repentance, Jesus will be sent back to them, at the times of the "restoration of all things"(the fortunes of Israel). It is another way of saying what Jesus said on His last speech in the temple, "Behold your house is left unto you desolate. For I say unto you, Ye shall not see me henceforth, till ye shall say, Blessed is he that comes in the name of the Lord" (Matthew 23:38-39). The other place and context of that word "restore" is in the rest of the first chapter of Acts, verse 6, where the apostles ask, "Lord, wilt thou at this time restore again the kingdom to Israel?" Note that the Lord would have had an excellent opportunity to give them the correct meaning of the restoration of all things, supposedly as applying to the "restoration" of the church, and not Israel, but He didn't. The apostles were right. Restoration, both New Testament and Old, applies to Israel, not the church.

However, the interpretation of Acts 3:20-21 has evolved along with Isaiah 43 and the passages that speak of the latter rain. Instead of Israel (and the church) awaiting the times of restoration of all things, "which the Father hath put in His own power" (Acts 1:7), the new interpretation is that it is now the Father and Jesus Christ who are waiting for us, the church, to complete its own restoration! For example, Earl Paulk states in his book, *The Wounded Body of Christ*, that we the church:

> Have been foreordained of God to become that people who will become so gloried (glorified?) that we can bring Christ back to the earth. This gloried (glorified?) church must make the earth God's footstool before Jesus can come again.[2]

Paulk states plainly that Jesus can't come back until we get it together. He is supposedly "held in the heavens" awaiting the church to restore all things. In this view, before the church can restore anything else, she must be restored herself, having lost the glory and power God intended to have her walk in, down through the Ages. Supposedly, now the church is doing it, as we are supposedly in continuous restoration, starting with Luther, who restored justification by faith; then Wesley, who restored sanctification; then Dowie, with his proclamations of divine healing; and on down to the "revival" at Azusa Street, with its proclamation of the Baptism of the Holy Ghost and speaking in tongues. According to the restorationist worldview, the church is progressing, as other facets of Christianity are being restored. Ah, but there is much more to come before Jesus can return! In the last few decades we've seen the church's focus on, spiritual warfare, deliverance, prayer marching, open churches, Davidic worship, etc. With the advent of the modern prophetic movement, of primary importance is the restoration of the "five-fold ministry" especially the last two offices—that of the apostle and the prophet. It is believed that under the "apostolic and prophetic" anointings, the church will finally perfect herself, and become a "glorious church, without spot or wrinkle" and be built upon the foundation of the (new) apostles and prophets, of course, with Christ Jesus being the chief cornerstone.

These were the presuppositions that were swirling around the Pentecostal world in the late 1940s, supplanting the other-worldly hope of the *Parousia*, the bodily return of Jesus. Powerful and well received sign gift ministries such as that of William Branham (whom I will speak of in the next chapter), Jack Coe, A. A. Allen, and Oral Roberts seemed to herald the dawn of a new day of power and anointing, the prophetic fulfillment of which was just around the corner.

Another influence in Pentecostal circles was a little book called *Atomic Power with God Through Fasting and Prayer*, which purported to teach the secret of immortality and increased anointing through extended fasting. The popularity of that book attests to the hunger for power that had developed in the churches.

In the late 1940s, ironically, at another "airport fellowship" in Canada, at a combination Bible school, orphanage, and church called the Sharon Home, George Hawtin and Percy Hunt, both heavily influenced by both Branham and the book, *Atomic Power with God Through Fasting and Prayer*, began praying and preaching a coming "latter rain." After a season of united prayer and fasting at the Bible school, a prophecy came forth in one of the classes. It, in effect, proclaimed the beginning of the "new thing"—that God would restore to the church the gifts of the Spirit and ministries of the apostles and the prophet, and that gifts and ministries would be "imparted" by the laying on of hands by those vessels whom God would so designate. Classes were canceled, the prayer meeting was extended, the word leaked out, and crowds began to gather. By that summer, thousands from all over the world had gathered for a camp meeting in Saskatchewan, Canada, seeking the new anointing. This was the genesis of what became known as the Latter Rain Revival. William Menzies, who wrote the official history of the Assemblies of God, *Anointed to Serve*, summarized the new thing this way:

In 1947, George Hawtin and Percy Hunt launched

an independent Bible school in North Battleford, Saskatchewan . . . They evolved a teaching that emphasized extreme congregationalism with local authority committed to a restored order of apostles having received a special dispensation derived through the laying on of hands, could in turn dispense a variety of spiritual gifts. Their extravagant claims and their belligerent attack on existing Pentecostal groups brought open conflict. Many sincere Christians followed the new group, which boasted of being a fresh revival displacing the apostatized Pentecostals.[3]

The characteristics Menzies outlined are interesting because the issues of "impartation," personal prophecies, restored apostles and prophets, belligerent attacks on existing Pentecostals, and extravagant claims have been the consistent pattern ever since the late 1940s. Impartation of anointing is what we are seeing currently. This practice reached its recent heyday in both the Toronto and Pensacola revivals of the 1990s, where people were literally embarking on pilgrimages in the hopes of receiving "the anointing." During that time, belligerent attacks on existing Pentecostals could be easily seen by those constant references to the established church as being "Jezebel," "Saul," dead religion, and "the accuser of the brethren."

As in the late 1940s, a good many Pentecostal churches have been broken up as the new apostles and prophets seek to draw disciples after themselves after downgrading the leadership of the established churches. You might notice that the new breed of prophets and apostles never seem to miss an opportunity to mock and castigate "religious deadheads," "Jezebel spirits," "Old Order" people, all of which are the names they use to refer to those who dare question the orthodoxy of practices such as "holy laughter," spiritual drunkenness, and other such manifestations.

As for "extravagant claims" as Menzies called them, there have been many. We are the generation, supposedly, in which "all of the purposes of God are wrapped up in," the believers will walk in "unprecedented levels of power and authority," whole nations will "tremble at the mention of their [new apostles and prophets] names," and these new prophets will be sought out by the "Presidents, the pharaohs, and the Babylonian emperors of this world." One of our current new prophets has been shown that in the end they will be saying (of them) "He [God] saved the best for last."

Menzies' quote gives us the Assemblies of God view (at the time of this book's first printing of the Latter Rain. J. Preston Eby, a Latter Rain teacher, gives a more favorable view of the movement when he states:

> In 1948, the very year Israel became a nation, another great deluge fell from heaven, a mighty revival called "The Latter Rain." In this restoration revival, God did a work which far transcended the . . . Pentecostal outpouring of forty years before. All nine gifts of the spirit, the fivefold ministries of apostles, prophets, evangelists, pastors, and teachers, spiritual praise and worship, and end-time revelation of God's purpose to Manifest His Sons, a glorious church, to bring in the Kingdom of God, all of this and much more was restored among God's people.[4]

The phrase "Manifested Sons of God," which Eby referred to, comes from Romans 8:19, and the "revelation" which Eby referred to, became the name of a sub-movement which sprang out of the Latter Rain. "For the earnest expectation of the creature waiteth for the manifestation of the sons of God," has long been interpreted as referring to the bodily return of Jesus Christ, to reverse the "curse of futility" imposed on the creation by God at the fall. At His coming, the lion will lay down with the lamb, and the meek (the sons of God, the believers) will be gloried for all to see.

In the "revelation of sonship," Romans 8:19 is seen as something that an elite company of believers attains to, through progressive revelation of "who we are in Christ." All of this sin-cursed creation awaits not the *Parousia*, but the coming into a glorification of an elite remnant of Christians! These Manifested Sons are glorified through progressive revelation of their "sonship." The Manifested Sons are seen as Christ. In this error the identity of Jesus Christ and the identity of the Body of Christ, the church, are confused. Some MSOG teachers even refer to an "ongoing incarnation of Christ," and imply that Christ has to come within us before He can ever come unto us. Prerogatives and responsibilities assigned to the resurrected Lord Jesus Christ alone have been assumed by those who have believed this error.

> At that time the sons of God will be fully manifested on the earth. Widespread spiritual warfare will result with the sons of God doing battle with Satan and company, the non-Christian nations of this world will also be defeated. Once the earth has been subdued, Jesus will come back to earth and be given the Kingdom that has been won for Him by this "manchild company." The Manifested Sons of God doctrine teaches that these sons will be equal to Jesus Christ: immortal, sinless, perfected sons who have partaken of the divine nature. They will have every right to be called gods and will be called gods.[5]

What a perversion of 1 Corinthians 15:24-28! It is HE, Jesus, who will "put down all rule and all authority and power," and HE also, who must "put all enemies under his feet," and HE who after accomplishing all of this Himself, will turn it all over to the Father, that "God may be all in all." HE is Jesus, not we the church. You can see, very quickly, the confusion of these two identities, and that confusion has begun to permeate the church.

Supposedly, the Manifested Sons of God will even be able, without the bodily return of Christ, to overcome even death! Paulk again, states:

The last enemy to be conquered is death. Who will conquer it? A mature church will come forth, with the kind of authority and power that will be able to stand in the very face of Satan. When the church reaches that level of maturity, God will be able to say, 'This generation of the church does not need to die. She has reached the place of maturity, I will translate her because her maturity pleases me.'[6]

Such a magnificent destiny is not reserved for all of the church, mind you, but only for the elite remnant, also known as either the Overcomers, the Manchild, the Joseph Company, and so forth. This whole movement appeals to elitism, the desire to be distinct, as Jude said, "These be they who separate themselves." For years the people of God have been steadily conditioned to think in terms of levels, such as "30 fold Christians, 60 and 100 fold saints," or "outer court, inner court, and Holy of Holies Christians." There is the "traditional church" as opposed to "the Manchild company," "the bride company," the "advancing church," "the prophetic church" and so forth. This, in a nutshell, is the flattering (?) heresy permeating the Pentecostal and Evangelical world, the idea that without the *Parousia* we can perfect ourselves into the "greatest expression of the church ever seen."

Besides the ongoing revelation, and the ministries of apostles and prophets, the only other way of being "gloried" and brought into full "sonship" is through impartations of the presence of God. It is this "presence" that many are seeking in their pilgrimages to various cities. God is, supposedly, "incarnating His Church." It is also known as the Glory, or the New Anointing. Many who have been to Toronto, Pensacola, Anaheim Vineyard, Rick Joyner meetings and other venues, have seen this "glory" as a silver cloud or at times as a bluish haze. As Jude says "These be they who separate themselves, sensual . . ." (v19).

This new anointing is what has spawned a host of chartered buses, pilgrimages little different from the Catholic pilgrimages to Lourdes and other Marion sites. Rather than waiting patiently for the *Parousia* of our Lord Jesus Christ, who alone will undo the curse on this earth and glorify His saints, these neo-gnostics cherish a different hope,which is their own attainment of glorification. According to these new prophets, the church herself will be presenting the earth, which she has conquered, unto Jesus.

Also there is an anointing (Christ) that has not come unto us in the flesh, but that gets us drunk, gives us visions and ultimately, deifies us. As one friend of mine put it, after "seeking the new anointing" as far back as 1960, she and her husband tired of "chasing the Charismatic carrot on a stick," and accepted the glorious realization that all we have needed has been given unto us in Christ, and it is in Him that we are to put our hope. These series of "revivals" are nothing new. There are many who have for years been listening to the same kind of prophecies, and been just as willing as anyone else to run to the next meeting, seeking the "new thing" or "more" from the Lord, believing the Great Revival is just around the corner.

THIS IS A BRIEF overview of the theology of the new prophetic movement. Others have done a more thorough treatment of it. I'm thinking of Al Dager's book, *Vengeance is Ours*, (Sword Publishing, PO Box 290, Redmond, WA, 98073-0290) which gives a more thorough treatment of the doctrine and its implications. In the 1940s, instead of imminent glory, the Latter Rain/Manifested Sons of God was reproached. The Assemblies of God repudiated the doctrine and practices, and the movement went into a forty year wilderness (as they see it). It would not entirely die out. The basic doctrines went forth under different names and through other vessels. Alternately, the Neo-Pentecostal Movement, the Word of Faith, Dominionism, Kingdom Now, The Sonship Message, The Walk, Shepherding and Accountability, Restorationism, and much of the Charismatic movement were used as vessels for the doctrines and teachings of this heresy down through the last forty years. It would not be until the late 1980s that the leavening had caused the MSOG doctrine to flower forth in full expression, through the Kansas City Prophets, Paul Cain, and the Vineyard Movement. For many, the one hope that the false concept of "sonship" was valid was in the memory of an archetypical "son" who it seemed to have worked for. In the hierarchy of the new prophetic kingdom, William Branham stands on one of the tallest pedestals. In order to further understand the new prophetic movement, one must consider his unusual story.

3

The Model Prophet

HE WAS A LITTLE boy in the hills of Kentucky, gravely disappointed as he thought of his friends playing ball while he was stuck "packing water" for the family. As he toted the heavy buckets, he heard a sound in the top of a poplar tree like that of a whirlwind. This was strange, for there was no breeze evident anywhere else. But strange occurrences were nothing new to this little boy; his whole life seemed marked by them. Suddenly, he heard an audible voice which instructed him, "Don't you ever drink, smoke or defile your body in any way. There will be work for you when you are older." Although this frightened young William Branham, it was only one of a number of remarkable occurrences in the life of this poor and uneducated Kentucky boy. Even his birth seemed blazoned with an otherworldly mark. His own words reveal much of both how he viewed himself, and how he portrayed himself to others:

> A light come whirling through the window, about the
> size of a pillow, and circled around where I was and
> went down on the bed.[1]

The friends and neighbors who supposedly witnessed the sight were awestruck. Gordon Lindsay, who wrote a biography of William Branham, begins in this fashion:

The story of the life of William Branham is so out of this world and beyond the ordinary that were there not available a host of infallible proofs which document and attest its authenticity, one might well be excused for considering it farfetched and incredible. But the facts are so generally known, and of such a nature that they can easily be verified by any sincere investigator, that they stand as God's witness to His willingness and purpose to reveal Himself again to men as He once did in the days of the prophets and the apostles. The story of this prophet's life-for he is a Prophet . . . indeed witnesses to the fact that Bible days are here again.[2]

Wow! This man left quite an impression on the people of his time! This introduction to Lindsay's book reads like the introduction to the Gospel of Luke! Branham still leaves an impression, even on a new generation. Paul Cain, Bob Jones, Rodney Howard Browne, Kenneth Copeland, Kenneth Hagin and many other current and past leaders in the charismatic movement speak extremely highly of Branham, in many cases as a true and great prophet of God. He is credited with being the father of the Latter Rain Revival. His teachings led to the Manifested Sons of God doctrine and to the Word of Faith teaching, and for our present purposes, the current prophetic movement owes much to the influence of this man.

Who is William Branham and why is he important to our discussion? As stated earlier, Branham's whole life was marked by a series of supernatural or paranormal experiences from his birth. As he put it one time:

There was always that peculiar feeling, like someone standing near me, trying to say something to me, and especially when I was alone. No one seemed to understand me at all.[3]

If his personal testimony is to be believed, even as an unconverted teenager, Branham's purity was safeguarded, for at critical moments of temptation, he would hear the sound of the whirling breeze and remember the instructions of the "voice." Eventually, Branham married, was converted, and even became a Baptist minister. At a public baptism administered by Branham, it was claimed that 4000 people witnessed a light shining down on Branham and that some heard the voice tell him that he would be as John the Baptist, a forerunner of the second coming of Christ. According to the story, many who witnessed this ran in fear, and many others worshiped. Eventually, when Branham was about forty years old, he had a crisis experience in which he fasted and prayed and sought the answer to the "presence" and the "voice" which had accompanied him all his life. After some hours in a cabin out in the woods, Branham relates:

> Then along in the night, at about the eleventh hour, I had quit praying and was sitting up when I noticed a light flickering in the room. Thinking someone was coming with a flashlight, I looked out the window, but there was no one, and when I looked back, the light was spreading out on the floor and getting wider . . . as I looked up there hung that great star . . . it looked more like a ball of fire or light shining down upon the floor . . . coming through the light, I saw the feet of a man coming toward me . . . He appeared to be a man who, in human weight would weigh about two hundred pounds, clothed in a white robe. He had a smooth face, no beard, dark hair down to his shoulders, rather dark complected with a very pleasant countenance . . . Seeing how fearful I was he said,

> Fear not. I am sent from the presence of the almighty God to tell you that your peculiar life and your misunderstood ways have been to indicate that God

has sent you to take a gift of divine healing to the people of the world. If you will be sincere and can get the people to believe you, nothing shall stand before your prayers, not even cancer.[4]

The angel went on to proclaim to him the twofold gifting ordained for Branham. He continued:

One of them will be that you will take the person that you are praying for by the hand with your left hand and their right, then just stand quiet and . . . there'll be a physical effect that'll happen on your body . . . then you pray, and if it leaves, the disease is gone from the people. If it doesn't leave then just ask a blessing and walk away.[5]

The other gift would allow Branham to know the "secrets of men's hearts." The angel also promised Branham that, "I will be with you and the gift will grow greater and greater."

Branham was catapulted from almost complete obscurity to international fame by holding whole auditoriums and even stadiums spellbound through the exercise of these two "sign gifts." This ministry, along with an explosion of those by other healing evangelists, was to give the Pentecostal movement a tremendous boost in the 1940s and 1950s.

But there was one big problem with Branham's ministry—his teachings.

Branham was discouraged from teaching by many in the Pentecostal movement with the admonition, "Just stick with the signs and wonders, the words of knowledge, and the healings." Why? Well, because as soon as Branham began to share what he actually believed, it made many people nervous. For example, Branham believed the doctrine known as the "Serpent's Seed" teaching. This heresy teaches that the Fall came about when Eve commenced a sexual relationship with Lucifer, thus putting the blame on woman. Out of that illicit union was born Cain, and through his descent has come the "wicked," which are with us to this day. Branham also propagated the heretical "Oneness" views and even stated that the doctrine of the Trinity was "of the devil." He believed in the dispensational view of the seven churches of the Book of Revelation, to wit, that these are seven epochs in church history. But his twist to this was that he was the Angel (Messenger) of the seventh church, Laodicea. He prophesied that the Rapture would occur in 1977, and taught that the Bible, the Zodiac, and the Egyptian pyramids were all forms of the Word of God.[6] When asked if it was the Holy Spirit Who performed his many signs and wonders, Branham replied, "NO, I do them by my Angel."

In truth, by his own admission, Branham was as helpless as a baby without his angel. Branham denied an eternal Hell and taught that denominationalism was the mark of the beast. The Word of Faith teaching, that reality can be created by the spoken word, and the basic teaching of the Manifested Sons of God, both have their beginnings in the belief system of Branham.

There is so much more I could say about this unique man, who had such a widespread impact on the Pentecostal and Charismatic world. Branham, on several occasions, was seen by even hostile witnesses to have a halo!! There are two photos, one taken by a hostile photographer hired by a man bent on exposing Branham as a false prophet, which when developed showed a halo over his head. This photo, reproduced in Gordon Lindsay's book, also has a certified letter from an investigator of questionable documents assuring the public that nothing had been done to tamper with the film. How do you question a man with a halo?

Not everyone accepted Branham as a prophet of God. Kurt Koch, a respected evangelical scholar who specialized in the study of the occult and demon possession, featured Branham in his book, *Between Christ and Satan*, where he wrote:

The question of discernment is of great importance, especially in the field of miracles. There are some miracle healers whose work is so hard to evaluate that Christians are often in doubt as to the forces behind these people. We have today for example men such as Tommy Hicks, Harry Edwards, T. L. Osborn and William Branham. Each one of these men depends on mass meetings which are followed by a call to people to step forward for healing. I have, over the years, collected a lot of information on these particular people and the conclusions that I have come to are not based on a superficial judgment of the matter . . . I have compared their teachings with the Holy Scriptures. My aim is to obey the plain meaning of the Bible, which tells us to "Try the spirits, to see whether they are from God" . . . the man who poses us with the most problems is Branham. He not only exhibits abilities of fortune telling, mesmerism, and magic, but he also has certain Christian characteristics. His whole work is hidden behind a screen of Christian words and phrases. Both his parents believed in fortune telling and he was burdened with occultism at an early age. He once told an audience . . . that he had visionary experiences since childhood . . . My comment is that the gifts of the Spirit are not imparted to a person at birth, but they receive them after their spiritual rebirth.[7]

Koch relates an example of the gift in operation in Zurich when he wrote:

He called a young man to the platform. He then asked the young man, "Do we know each other?" "No," was the reply. Branham went on to say, "Have you got a letter in your pocket from a young lady?" this time the answer was, "Yes." "There is a picture with the letter." "That's right." "Will you show me the picture?" The young man pulled it out and Branham held it out for all . . . to see. "Am I not a prophet?" he called out. There was an enthusiastic response from the people together with cries of "Hallelujah" and "Praise the Lord!" But we ask, is a piece of fortune telling proof of one's prophetic ability? There should be no confusion here, as the Bible points out, fortune telling is of the devil (Acts 16:16)."[8]

Branham died at 56 years old in a head-on auto collision in 1965. Some of his followers were so sure he would rise from the dead, they put off burying him for quite some time. In 1961, the Full Gospel Businessmen's Association's *Voice* magazine said this of Branham:

> In Bible days, there were men of God who were prophets and seers, but in all the sacred records, none of these had a greater ministry than that of William Branham.

The Word of Faith Movement, the Manifested Sons of God, and the current Prophetic movement are all part of the legacy and influence of this one man, William Branham. Though he was eventually regarded with suspicion because of his erratic teachings, many have been enamored and directly influenced by him, and these are now influencing hundreds of thousands of this generation who don't really know anything but good about William Branham. After all, he had the power, didn't he? As Al Dager says in his excellent book, *Vengeance is Ours*:

> William Branham's body is still in the grave. But his occult methodology of healing was picked up by hundreds of pastors and teachers upon whom he laid his hands and who have traded on it to a greater or lesser degree.[9]

Mike Oppenheimer of Let Us Reason Ministries explains the lasting effect Branham has had on modern-day Christianity:

> There are few men who have affected the Church in modern times in such a way that after almost 40 years, ministries still model themselves after and speak of in an adoring fashion. . . . William Branham is always mentioned as possibly the greatest. You can say Branham was the light at the beginning of the tunnel for Pentecostal healing and miracle meetings.[10]

4

The Decades of the Prophets

The eighties revealed my prophets you see, and the nineties revealed my government and my justice, even improving on this day . . . And yes my good shepherds that are coming out of many places, they will put to rest the troubled waters in the church . . . They will have authority to speak against those that lie, the gossips, the slanderers, those that trouble the waters.[1]

As we have looked at earlier, according to the theology of the Latter Rain/Manifested Sons of God, the church cannot come into her glory until the prophetic and apostolic anointings are restored, for it is they who will come on the scene to bring divine order and authority to the church. As one prominent prophetic leader has declared:

The company of prophets will help restore the apostles back into their rightful place in the church. The full restoration of apostles and prophets back into the church will bring divine order, unity, purity, and maturity to the corporate Body of Christ.[2]

In the late 1980s, the "prophetic" seemed to begin breaking forth and not just on an isolated scale. A Pentecostal church in Kansas City, known simply at that time as the Kansas City Fellowship, became world-renowned as a laboratory for the development of the prophetic ministry. It was centered around a band of men who were to become known as the Kansas City Prophets. The young, earnest, pastor, Mike Bickle, had, on a trip to Cairo, Egypt, heard an audible voice tell him:

> I am inviting you to raise up a work that will touch the ends of the earth. I have invited many people to do this thing and many people have said yes, but very few have done my will.[3]

The "work" that Bickle had been invited to raise up was a seven-faceted amalgamation of various traveling prophetic and apostolic ministries dedicated to church planting and intercession. The seven facets were: apostolic teams, city churches, the House of Prayer, the Joseph Company, the Israel Mandate, a ministry training center, and Shiloh ministries, which was a type of retreat and training center bringing novice and experienced prophets together for ministry.

Before long, Kansas City Fellowship had become internationally known as a prophetic center. Bickle had surrounded himself with a band of prophets who, for the most part, taught and prophesied the old Manifested Sons themes. An outstanding example of this is found in the tapes from the church titled, "Visions and Revelations," which were soon distributed across the English speaking world. The tapes consist of Bickle interviewing prophet Bob Jones. Bickle draws out of Jones his testimonies of countless mystical experiences, dreams, visions, revelations, and demonic attacks on his person. Bickle would make a perfect character for a Frank Peretti book! The following is a mere sampling of the theology of those involved:

> You know, I'm going to tell you something about Bob [Jones]. Ever since that time he was led with the Holy Spirit in '74 he began to see Technicolor visions and the Lord began to visit him . . . He has five or ten visions

and dreams a night!—Mike Bickle[4]

There is a lingo that one must adopt to understand the terms and concepts of the prophets, and it is the terminology of the Latter Rain/Manifested Sons of God. It constantly speaks of "birthing" and bringing forth the Bride. It assumes personalities such as Jezebel and Elijah, are currently in conflict (spiritually, allegorically). In this view, the manchild of Revelation 12 has yet to come forth and, as is the case with all gnostics, soon the symbolic assumes more reality than the real. From the same tape, we have Bob Jones asserting:

> The Last Days church is being birthed out of the old church, and the old leadership is coming to an end and the new, young leadership is being raised up to reign over an end time church that will bring forth the bride.[5]

What exactly is he saying here? One would have to be conditioned to think allegorically in order to understand this. It goes back to the Latter Rain attacks on the existing church that Menzies wrote of. "The old church," in this thinking, is like Saul. And Jones prophesies that the "old leadership" is coming to an end to make room for the new, a kind of Saul-and-David scenario. In this prophecy, one also learns that the Bride hasn't even "come forth" yet. This is an example of the elite concept. Not all Christians qualify to be the Bride nor the saints down through time, for the Bride supposedly is to be "birthed" in the Last Days church. The worldwide appeal of this tape is mystifying. It could only be a spiritual phenomenon that so many in the Pentecostal and charismatic churches (not to mention many evangelicals churches as well) were enamored by this tape.

Apparently, Jones has a standing appointment with the Lord, for on the Day of Atonement, the Lord comes to "stand before" Jones yearly. Also, Jones inaugurated an annual day of judgment in the church, described in another Jones/Bickle interview, titled "The Shepherd's Rod." On this day, Bickle and the whole church passed under the prophet's shepherd's rod for an annual inspection of the fruit of their lives! Is any of this based on the teachings of the apostles as normative standards of Christianity? Did the apostles have personal annual appointments with Jesus on holy feast days? This is Jones's personal private revelation knowledge that he claims came to him, obviously unmediated. In other words, he is a gnostic, who has broken into some mystical experiences, and been accepted as a prophet of God!

We are told by one who could actually boast of some really valid spiritual experiences that, "no prophecy of the scripture is of private interpretation" (2 Peter 1:20). The one who was actually on the Mount of Transfiguration with Jesus, Moses, and Elijah would offer to us the "more sure word of prophecy" (2 Peter 1:19) and would warn us to beware of the "false teachers among you . . . who privily shall bring in damnable heresies" and secretly lay truth alongside of error" (see 2 Peter 1:16-2:2). Yes, there is indeed a Day of Atonement, but no, Jones doesn't have an actual standing appointment with the Lord of Glory, annually on that day!

Earlier, Menzies also spoke of the "extravagant claims" of the Latter Rain proponents, which are echoed in the Bickle/Jones tapes:

> Mike Bickle: "He [God] said, 'I'll cause 300,000 to bear a distinct anointing over the one billion [converts] . . . They will have a special measure of the Spirit . . . there is one generation that will enter into that beyond all others. The chosen generation of history that will go beyond all others in power.'"

> Bob Jones: "From out of the sands of time I [God] have called the best of every bloodline in the earth unto this generation . . . Even the bloodline of Paul. Even the bloodline of David, the bloodline of Peter, James, and John. The best of their seed is unto this generation. They will even be superior to them in heart, stature, and love for me."

It never ceases to amaze me that such blatant error is overlooked by the thousands and thousands who have so eagerly embraced the Kansas City Prophets. The anticipation for the "new thing"—the Latter Rain, Great Last Days Revival—that the Manifested Sons of God, charismatic, and Word of Faith teachers have conditioned so many for, has effectively blinded so many. When the word spread that there were "prophets" in the land, Kansas City became in the 1980s what North Battleford, Saskatchewan, Canada was in the summer of 1948, what Toronto became in 1994, and what Pensacola became a year after that. These places, and many others since then, have all become a form of Mecca for tens of thousands from around the world who are seeking the new anointing.

Among the many who came to behold were John Wimber and Paul Cain. Wimber, at one-time the head of the Vineyard Movement, quickly became enamored with the prophets and embraced their ministry, giving them further worldwide exposure. Another who was drawn to their light was Paul Cain, also a prophet and a former associate minister to William Branham who had retired from public prophetic ministry after being disillusioned by the greed he saw there. He had felt called by God to leave the limelight to enter a simple life, "marked by Bible study and prayer."

Jones and Bickle, in their widely distributed interviews, whetted an appetite in many for mystical experiences, in which Jones's ministry abounds. These include the appearance of a spirit named Dominus who, according to Jones, is Jesus; his encounters with a talking white horse; and demonic attacks which left gashes on his arms. As Bickle explained:

> Bob Jones has come to me several times after ministry . . . you may not believe this . . . where he went to bed at night and woke up in the morning with a big red streak across his face or a big cut, a gash, on his arm. He'd say, "They got me last night," he was at warfare in the realm of trances and visions and there was marks left on his body.[6]

Jones could even tell Bickle what dreams he was going to have, as well as come to him in his dreams! Like Branham, Jones confesses to being burdened with the paranormal at an early age. Once, Jones was hit by lightening and out of that experience he developed "Golden Senses," the ability to feel in his hands and arms sensations that would signal various spiritual realities. Mike Bickle touches on this when he said:

> Bob . . . we talked about the golden senses because you said that the Lord is going to be . . . touching the senses . . . the Lord visited Bob, I think in '75 and touched him by the Spirit of God . . . the phrase Bob uses is his senses turn golden, that means his five physical senses literally were inspired by the Holy Spirit . . . He could tell what was happening in the Spirit realm . . . there's twenty or thirty different signs that show up in his body.[7]

This is the kind of thing which drew literally thousands of seekers to Kansas City and inaugurated the 1980s as the prophetic decade.

Paul Cain, to whom I made reference earlier, as a young man in the 1940s and 1950s was a rising star in the Latter Rain movement, as well as was his protégé William Branham, whom he called "The Greatest Prophet Ever." But he became disillusioned by the greed and pride he saw in the ministry, so he retired into semi-seclusion. Cain believed God showed him to wait this way until the rise of the "New Breed" of men and women leaders who would be known by their "simplicity, purity, and remarkable manifestations of power." It was in a 1987 meeting with the leaders of the Kansas City Fellowship that Cain decided he had met his "New Breed." Bob Jones bore witness to Cain, calling him the "Terror of the Lord or the Jealousy of God." This strong impression may have come about because of some of Cain's predictions, such as this one recorded in Al Dager's Media Spotlight article:

Jack Deere, a Vineyard Pastor, stated that in 1989 Cain told him an earthquake would occur on the same day Cain arrived for the first time to meet John Wimber at the Vineyard Church in Anaheim, California. Another would occur on the day he left Anaheim. According to Deere, Cain said the earthquake would be a confirmation that the Lord had a strategic purpose for the Vineyard Movement. A relatively minor earthquake common to Southern California shook Pasadena on the day Cain arrived. Cain claims that on the day after he left Anaheim, the Soviet-Armenian Earthquake occurred. But the records show that it occurred while Cain was still in Anaheim.[8]

Another attestation to Cain's validity, in many people's minds, were the power surges that occurred at auditoriums where he held his meetings, blowing fuses, setting off fire alarms, and even short- circuiting video cameras! In one case, a battery-operated video camera was surged and short-circuited! Bickle may well have been referring to this when, after the outbreak of the Toronto Blessing, he attempted to help those who were experiencing various manifestations by publishing a paper titled, "God's Manifest Presence, Understanding the Phenomenon that Accompany the Spirit's Ministry," which catalogued such manifestations—

> [S]haking, jerking, loss of bodily strength, heavy breathing, eyes fluttering, lips trembling, oil on body, changes in skin color . . . drunkenness . . . visions, hearing audibly into the spirit realm . . . jumping, violent rolling, screaming, nausea as discernment of evil, smelling or tasting good or evil presence . . . feeling heavy weight or lightness, trances . . . disruption into the natural realm, i.e. circuits blown.[9]

Amazingly, all of the above and more were presented as having been "observed in contemporary experience." They also happen to be the same types of symptoms experienced during the occultic kundalini experience!

Like Jones and the other Kansas City Prophets, Cain held forth the standard Manifested Sons of God message—the birthing of the "new breed" of elite overcomers who would walk in power and glory hitherto unknown in church history. They would purge the Old Order, and bring in the New Order, led by apostles and prophets. They would become the much-touted Joel's Army. In a taped message, Paul Cain stated:

> You know this army . . . is also in the New Testament. It's referred to as the Manchild, Rev 12:5 . . . the overcomers, Rev 2 and 3, the 144,000 servants, Rev. 7:3, the Bride or the Lamb's wife . . . the White Horse, Rev 6:2, the first fruits . . . the precious fruits . . . the wise virgins . . . the Manifested Sons of God . . . and it's really remarkable . . . that none of these names are expressions applied to the saints of God or at any other time in history . . . they belong to this present generation . . . God's offering to the believers of this generation a greater privilege than was ever offered to any people of any generation at any time from Adam all the way down to the Millennium.[10]

Cain, in the manner of Branham, Jones, Bill Hamon, Rick Joyner, and others constantly prophesies a redefinition of Christianity based on the ministry of new prophets and apostles, which he calls, "the prize of all the ages." He states:

> I think the most wonderful thing God is doing for us in these last days is raising up and restoring completely apostolic leadership, apostolic authority . . . the hope of the church, the hope of the world, is the apostolic ministry . . . So here God is raising up a new standard, a new banner, if you will, that's going to radically change

the expression, the understanding of Christianity in our generation . . . God has invited us to have a role in establishing this New Order of Christianity . . . God is offering to this generation something He has never offered to any other generation before. He's giving us an open invitation to participate in something that will lead to the prize of all the ages . . . It's greater than anything He's ever done from Adam clear down through the millennium.[11]

It's flattering to hear prophecies that set us up as the "greatest generation," so great that nothing God has done down through time, until now, compares with it. This flattery has disarmed countless church goers who are seeking meaning for their lives.

By the early '90s, the Kansas City Prophets had begun to lose their luster, as their many false prophecies, wrong predictions, and the fallout in the lives of many who had been influenced by their "words," began to filter out. The Network of Christian Ministries was in the process of actually setting up a meeting to hold the Kansas City Prophets accountable on the basis of a paper written by a prominent Kansas City pastor documenting their errant teachings and practices. Before this happened, in the interest of making peace, John Wimber stepped forward and offered to bring the prophets under his "covering." This is the same Wimber who had completely been enamored with them a short time earlier! The Kansas City Fellowship became the Metro Vineyard of Kansas City. Paul Cain still ministers worldwide. Bob Jones* was exposed shortly thereafter for sexual immorality and was asked to step down, though was later "rehabilitated" and again recognized as a prophet. John Paul Jackson still ministers in Streams Ministries International (which he founded), and Mike Bickle is recognized as an authority on the "prophetic," and in his 2008 book, *Growing in the Prophetic*, he said he still considered Bob Jones as a prophet of God. To illustrate the ludicrous kinds of "prophetic" display by these prophets, one particular prophecy of Jones's was that the Broncos would win the Super Bowl in 1998 because their quarterback was named Elway. As he stated:

> For my purpose is to get you to listen that I might show you El's Way . . . for you see in every thunderstorm, in every lightening strike, in every earthquake, in every volcano, I [God] have my way, for I AM ELWAY.[12]

Note: Bob Jones is not the Fundamentalist minister and Bible College founder, nor is he his son. As I explained in my other book, *Weighed and Found Wanting*, Bob Jones was an alleged prophet, prominent among the so-called "Kansas City Prophets." He died on February 14, 2014 at 84 years old.

5

Rick Joyner—Taking the Baton

What is about to come upon the earth is not just a revival or another awakening, it is a veritable revolution. This vision was given in order to begin awakening those who are destined to radically change the course and even the very definition of Christianity.[1]—Rick Joyner

Homosexuality is having relations with your own sex. "Spiritual Homosexuality" is also the desire to have relations only with your own kind. The Lord spelled this "homo-sect-uality." This is not meant to just be a funny play on words—it is a deadly serious condition in the church. Sectarianism is self-centeredness, self seeking, and self preservation that is the result of self-worship . . . Many of the world's great artists are homosexual. This lifestyle is so prevalent in the artistic community because, to a large degree, art as a true form of worship has been rejected by the church.[2]

THE EXPOSURE OF SOME of the false prophecies and errant practices of the Kansas City Prophets, and the subsequent disciplines imposed upon them by John Wimber, didn't chill the prophetic movement in any sense of the word. It only opened the door for the development of more prophetic ministries. It also served to further condition people to accept the idea of "prophets-in-training," not one hundred percent accurate as Moses insisted but evolutionary prophets, getting more accurate as they "practice" on people.

In 1989, at the height of the Kansas City Prophets phenomenon, *The Harvest: The Prophetic Word of the Nineties and Beyond*, a 224-page prophecy by Rick Joyner, made its debut. The Harvest foretold of a great move of the Spirit to come, and the things which must precede it. It included, of course, the complete dismantling of the "Old Order" (presumably meaning the old ecclesiastical order) to make room for the new. Joyner prophesied many warnings to leaders that:

> If the leaders resist this move, the Lord will continue to move through the congregations. These groups will begin to relate to other members of the Body of Christ and their bonds will grow stronger, regardless of the opposition from resistant pastors . . . the pastors and leaders who continue to resist this tide of unity will be removed from their place . . . Some that were greatly used of God in the past have become too rigid in doctrinal emphasis . . . to participate in this revival . . . Those who are linked together by doctrine or gathered around personalities will be quickly torn away . . . Some leaders will actually disband their organizations as they realize they are no longer relevant to what God is doing . . . A great company of prophets, teachers, pastors, and apostles will be raised up . . . This harvest will be so great that no one will be able to look back at the early church as a standard, all will be saying that the Lord saved the best for last.[3]

I have selected these excerpts because many familiar themes are contained in them. The repetition of these themes eventually becomes monotonous: the irrelevancy of many current ministries and their subsequent dismantling; the condemnation of those who have become "doctrinally rigid," contrasted to the coming "great company" of doctrinally tolerant five-fold ministries; the New Order/Old Order theme; and the standard exaltation of this coming breed of new Christian who will do mighty exploits far surpassing those of the Lord's New Testament apostles. You know, "the best saved for last." And, of course, no prophetic utterance is complete without the warning to those who would resist. Joyner stated:

> Some pastors . . . who continue to resist this tide of unity will be removed from their place. Some will be so hardened they will become opposers and resist God to the end . . . This is the year when the Lord starts to bring down the spirit of Jezebel. He will begin by calling her to repentance. Those who have been vessels for this Spirit and who do not repent will be displayed as so insane that even the most immature Christians will discern their sickness.[4]

Does this sound like the Lord of the church? Think! What is it that they are doing that could possibly bring this kind of judgment on them? We are not talking about Christ resisting communists here, nor satanists. This is a "prophecy" aimed at the shepherds of the Lord's flock! What did they do to bring insanity on themselves, so obvious that everyone can see it? Did they renounce their vows? Reject Jesus? Blaspheme from the pulpit? This threat is leveled at people who have given their life to serve Jesus' flock, often for no glory (and no gold) and their only sin was to reject this so called revival! This intimidation is effective enough, for these are tough times to be in the pastorate, especially if you happen to be shepherding a "little flock." The bluster of these supposed men of God who appear to be successful (by this world's standards), their arrogance, and "great swelling words" can be intimidating, in this day of outward appearances. And more than one pastor, toiling in obscurity, losing people who want to be "where the action is" have been swept into the revival against their better judgment. Therefore, those uttering these un-Christlike threats will be answerable before the Throne of God, where judges the True Shepherd!

And yet, out of the abundance of the heart, the mouth speaketh (and prophesies). That is why so much of the prophecy (when it is not attempting to bully people with threats) is about how great the modern apostles and prophets are. As *The Harvest* brings out—

> It was said of the Apostle Paul that he was turning the world upside down . . . it will be said of the apostles soon to be anointed that they have turned the world right side up. Nations will tremble at the mention of their name.[5]

No wonder the world looks upon much of the charismatic arm of the modern church as a refuge for fanatics or religious ideologues, who shun logical discourse and fuel their emotions with self-congratulatory fantasies. Did Peter and Paul want nations to tremble at the mention of their names? Did they go about prophesying of their exploits? Only in this self-absorbed generation would such a prophecy even remotely be considered as a word from God.

The theme of the rejection of the leadership of the "Old Order" of the church consistently recurs in this ministry, as in this prophecy, from a Harvest Conference:

> We are all members of one another and we must start acting like the church as a body . . . we have come to a time of spiritual revolution . . . Benjamin Franklin said "We've gotta join or die," is becoming increasingly applicable to the church, those who refuse to tear down the walls, I tell you the people are going to do it . . . And just as those of the former order who did not recognize that a new order had come upon the church— that there is a new order today . . . Some of the most penetrating scenes that I saw in the news last year were the communist leaders who . . . had been some of the

most powerful people in this world, were on their knees
begging the people to listen to them and the people were
saying, "Away with you we will never listen to you again."
A New Order has come, I tell you, you are going to see
the same things taking place in the church.[6]

What a vision! Who is this tyrannical enemy that is so cursed
that he will either be displayed as insane, or the people will
publically reject him, as they did cruel communist dictators like
Ceausescu? The answer? Pastors—often little appreciated, these
hard-working unknowns are often in danger of being abandoned
by fickle, entertainment-saturated people who are ever learning
and never coming to the knowledge of the truth. And what is the
crime that deserves such reproach as insanity or open and public
rejection? Why, the high crime of not going along with the "New
Order."

Joyner is very much active in the prophetic ministry to this
day. One of his greatest contributions to the modern prophetic
movement is *The Final Quest*, a thin but action-packed volume
published by Whitaker House. The 158-page prophecy contains
what Joyner refers to as "some strategic revelations." The visions
it contains are said to "illuminate some doctrines." His first vision
is titled "The Hordes of Hell are Marching." It describes a cosmic
battle in which the Army of God is arrayed against the Hordes of
Hell. The demonic army, in full battle array, rides not on horses,
but on the backs of "well dressed, respectable . . . and educated"
Christians. The vision describes the demons as vomiting, defecating, and urinating on the Christians, who mistook the above for
the "Truth of God" and for the "Anointing of the Holy Spirit!"
The battle that will soon come, Joyner says, will be known by
many as "The Great Christian Civil War." This American Civil
War motif has also been prophesied by James Ryle, Bob Jones,
Wes and Stacy Campbell, and other prophets. In the surreal world
of the prophets, symbolism takes on a life of its own. The "Blues"
in the army have been interpreted as those who are operating on

revelation knowledge, blue being symbolic of heaven. The "Grays" are still operating out of their heads (gray matter, the brain—get it?) The Gray Army (of Christians) are seeking to hold the church in "spiritual slavery."

In *The Final Quest's* horrifying portrayal of this spiritual war zone, a figure Joyner knows as the angel "Wisdom" guides Joyner through his vision. It makes for a good fantasy novel, full of interesting details such as talking eagles, ascending a multilevel mountain, and arrows which represent Bible truths. As Joyner ponders the meaning of his vision, he writes:

> A great Civil War now looms before the church . . . the Lord is now preparing a leadership that will be willing to fight a Civil War in order to set men free. The main issue will be slavery versus freedom . . . The church will not be destroyed, but the institutions and doctrines that have kept men in spiritual slavery will be. Even after this, perfect justice in the church will not be attained overnight. There will be struggles for women's rights and to set the church free from other forms of racism and exploitation.[7]

It would be helpful to know what Joyner and other "prophets" are specifically referring to when they accuse a good number of Christians of "spiritual slavery." And just what doctrines are these prophets crying out against? Add racism, exploitation, and oppression of women to the list of sins for which Joyner believes the "Old Order" is responsible. But posturing themselves as the Union Army, the new prophets aspire to be saviors, attaining "perfect justice." The only reason I think we should talk about these vain imaginations is because thousands of Christians have taken *The Final Quest* seriously!

This last observation should serve as an ominous warning to those of us who follow Christ. That so many are deceived, and happily so, indicates a widespread and alarming biblical illiteracy.

Jesus and the apostles, as well as the Old Testament prophets, took great care to warn of the inundation of false prophecies that would come to erode the truth and carry God's people away into the worship of false gods. And make no mistake—false prophecies alter the character of God to the point where He is no longer the God of the Bible. The deceived wind up worshiping a god of their own making, a god based on imaginings, vain thoughts, or unrestrained emotions. The New Testament books of First and Second Corinthians amply demonstrate that even genuine believers in Christ can be led astray by their own lusts, including the lust ("strong desire") to follow a charismatic but false leader rather than their Lord. The only remedy to keep from falling into this kind of deception is to know your Bible, to take it literally, and to stand strong in the Lord, no matter how persuasive a dream, vision, an emotion, or a prophet.

The remainder of *The Final Quest* reads like an apocryphal book. Much of it is dialogue is with Wisdom, who also came to Joyner in the form of a talking eagle. Joyner also is allowed to interview the apostle Paul, one of the reformers, and numerous departed saints. Through the talking eagle, Joyner is given such nuggets as the following:

> Even though you have climbed to the top of the mountain, and have received from every truth along the way, and even though you have stood in the garden of God, tasted of His unconditional love, and have seen His Son many times now, you still understand only a part of the whole counsel of God and that only superficially.[8]

The angel Wisdom also teaches Joyner and the church that:

> "The Lord dwells within. You have taught this many times but now must live it for you have eaten of the tree of Life." The Angel then began to lead me back to the gate (out of Paradise). I protested that I didn't want

to leave. Looking surprised, the Angel took me by the shoulders and looked me in the eyes, that is when I recognized him as the Angel Wisdom. "You never have to leave this garden, this garden is in your heart because the Creator Himself is within you."[9]

Joyner forces thinking Christians into a decision, for he is not saying, "I think it is like this" (allegorically), nor is he offering a controversial exegesis of Scripture, a personal viewpoint that would be debatable. No, he claims to have interacted with angels, had visions, talked to spiritual eagles who talked back to him and, like the mystics of old, climbed "the Holy Mountain." Either he is lying or telling the truth about his experiences. There is no reason to believe he is lying, therefore we can assume that he had these experiences. The question is, did Joyner actually speak to an angel of God? Did he receive from the Lord the vision of the "Hordes of Hell" defecating and vomiting on Christians? Because this man has been set forth as a prophet of God, loyalty to God demands that we take a critical look at his ministry.

Such unbelieveable atrocities are being embraced by far too many in the church. Former elder of a Latter Rain church, Kevin Reeves, summarizes this catastrophe. We would do well to heed his concerns:

> These are critical days for the body of Christ. We are in the epoch of church history spoken of by the apostle Paul as "perilous times" (2 Timothy 3:1). What makes the danger all the more imminent is that not much of the church believes it. Many of us have owned the glorious but erroneous vision of an end-times remnant walking in unconquerable power, transforming entire societies. The result has been nothing short of catastrophic. How soon we forget. Every cult in the world has sprouted from the fertile soil of deception, always initiated by a drastic move away from the primacy of the Word of God into the nebulous, self-defining atmosphere of experience.[10]

6

Why I Wouldn't Send Any Kids to IHOP

ONE OF THE MOST dynamic and controversial offshoots of the prophetic movement, is IHOP, which was founded by Mike Bickle. IHOP, the International House of Prayer is a movement dedicated to intercession, worship, missions and evangelism. It is all at once a church, a nonstop (15 year) 24/7 prayer meeting, a university, a yearly conference and a constant series of retreats aimed primarily at youth. Tens of thousands of young people have been directly impacted by IHOP.

I receive inquiries regularly from pastors and parents, asking me, "What is IHOP all about? Would you send your youth group or your son or daughter to it?" My answer is plain and simple: I wouldn't, under any circumstances allow any youth group or child to go to any of the retreats or conferences, the IHOP University, or any other of the training centers associated with IHOP. Let me get right to the point: I wouldn't send *anyone* to IHOP because it is founded upon a series of false prophecies and discredited prophets.

Mike Bickle claims his life has been directed by a series of supernatural experiences initiated by a "prophet" named Augustine. These experiences involve prophets, miracles, signs, wonders, dreams, visions, and revelations. I reported on this in my book *Weighed and Found Wanting: Putting the Toronto Blessing in Context*. In that book, I state:

Bickle originally had pastored in St. Louis. In June of 1982, a man named Augustine approached Bickle and told him that he had heard an audible voice telling him to prophesy by the "spirit of truth" to Bickle's congregation. Bickle allowed him to do this and was impressed by the seeming accuracy with which he described the condition of his church. In September, the same year, Mike Bickle himself heard an audible voice speak to him, while on a trip in Cairo, Egypt. The voice told him, I am inviting you to raise up a work that will touch the ends of the earth. I have invited many people to do this thing and many people have said yes, but very few have done my will.[1]

This is eerily similar to what the "angel" Moroni told Joseph Smith of the Mormon church, especially the part about how he had asked others to do what he was asking of Bickle, but Bickle alone would prove faithful.

The "prophet" Augustine led Bickle to other "prophets"—Bob Jones and Paul Cain, and eventually to the founding of Kansas City Fellowship. As the church grew, other "prophets and seers" gathered around Bickle and company, and began to prophesy and implement the Manifested Sons of God vision of restored apostles and prophets to surrounding churches and through ever growing conferences across the nation.

Through the late 1980s and into the early '90s, the fame of the Kansas City Prophets increased and the movement grew. Churches were sending for the "prophets," young people were being trained in "the prophetic," and the teachings and interviews of Mike Bickle were spread around the world.

But there were some disturbing reports circulating of "prophets" upsetting local churches through their authoritative "words," and of people being hurt by the movement. One young man at a Christian high school was called out by a "young prophet" in training and told before an assembly of the entire student body that he had a pornography problem. But he didn't.

Not only was the young man humiliated before a mixed audience of his peers, but the "prophet" himself, when he realized that he had born false witness, was put on a temporary suicide watch.

Eventually the scandal became too great. A local pastor in Kansas City, Ernie Gruen, produced a cassette tape titled "Shall we just keep smiling and saying nothing?" in which he documented many of the abuses, false teachings, and false prophecies of the Kansas City Prophets. This was reported in *Charisma Magazine* and led to demands for oversight of Bickle and his prophets.

As I mentioned in the previous chapter, John Wimber stepped forward and offered to become a disciplinary covering for Mike Bickle and KCF. Bickle accepted and in the process, changed the name of his church to Metro Vineyard of Kansas City. In July 1993 Bickle admitted to *Charisma*:

- We had an elite spirit. That's become more and more real to me—it's so repulsive.

- We promoted mystical experience in a disproportionate way and it was disastrous.

- We were careless in the way we communicated prophetic words. This was hurtful in a lot of cases.

- We were wrong in the way we promoted the city church concept. I still believe in it, but now I believe it's a unity based on friendship.

In 1994 after the Wimber intervention, I wrote in *Weighed and Found Wanting*:

> In following the trail of error that has led to this current mystic revival, we need to fully explore the role of the company of men known as the Kansas City Prophets. The controversy that surrounded them in the late 1980s

and very early 1990s seems to have died down since John Wimber came forward to offer them a "covering" through affiliation with the Vineyard Movement. It is my contention that instead of truly resolving the problems that were raised by these false prophets, a band-aid was put over the whole affair. The erroneous teaching and ministry of Paul Cain, Bob Jones, John Paul Jackson, and others has been promoted and circulated through the Body of Christ in the years since Vineyard has been their covering.

Bob Jones, (one of the more obviously false prophets) finally was exposed, but not as a false prophet, but for an ethical/moral failure. His prophecies have been cited several times as valid at Toronto Airport Vineyard. The very same people who heralded these men as prophets are now heralding this spiritual drunkenness as a great "end times" revival. Perhaps behind the scenes of this "latest move of the Spirit" there just might be some of the same people offering their "prophetic ministry." We are not talking about personality differences or about doctrinal hairsplitting. [These] men . . . have presumed to speak prophetically, in the name of the Lord, (as though God were talking) to the whole, universal church! They have made great claims, like "The Lord spoke to me clearly . . . " or "I stood face to face before the Lord."

And what is in the message? Sheer Manifested Sons, Latter Rain, last days Super Church, church as the "manchild" stuff, reheated, repackaged and rehashed! In describing the Kansas City Prophets, there are three men, Mike Bickle, Bob Jones, and Paul Cain who held the most prominence. It's also important, however, to take a fresh look at how the church handled (or failed to handle with responsibility) the exposure of false prophecy, for this has set the course which we are currently on, and the same people who wouldn't discern at that time, even more so now, refuse to think critically. [2]

IHOP Leadership's Praise of Sexual Deviants

I WOULDN'T SEND ANYONE to IHOP because the leadership has continually rehabilitated and praised false prophets even after they were exposed as sexual deviants.

But there was more scandal yet to break. Bob Jones was confronted and admitted to the sexual abuse of two women in the church. *Religion News Blog* reported on this:

> Bob Jones, an associate of the Olathe Worship Center of the Metro Vineyard Fellowship of Kansas City, confessed Saturday to sexual misconduct with two women, who attend a Vineyard church in the Kansas City area, said Kenn Gulliksen, North American coordinator for the Association of Vineyard Churches. Jones, 63, was removed from his church duties for an undetermined amount of time, Gulliksen said. [3]

The "undetermined amount of time" for Jones turned out to be five years. Rick Joyner took it upon himself to bring Jones back into ministry, and in a short time Jones was once again highly revered, and his false prophecies and dangerous doctrines were allowed to continue to spread until his death in 2014.

In another sledge hammer blow to the movement, in 1995 Paul Cain, the man the prophetic movement regarded as "The terror of the Lord," was confronted and admitted that he was an alcoholic and a homosexual, after Rick Joyner, Mike Bickle, and Jack Deere confronted him.

> "I have struggled with homosexuality for an extended period of time," Cain said in his written apology. "I have struggled with alcoholism for an extended period

of time. I apologize for denying these matters of truth,
rather than readily admitting them. I am ashamed of
what I have done to hurt those close to me and for
the pain I have caused those who have believed in my
ministry."[4]

One wonders if there was any soul searching, or self exam-
ination, or true curiosity among those who had so praised and
promoted these immoral men, foisting them on the church as
some kind of modern Jeremiah or Isaiah. Did anyone ask him
or herself, "Where was my discernment?" or "Have I ever really
heard from God?" or "Why am I so gullible?"

But as in the tale of the Emperor's non-existent clothes, the
movers and shakers of the prophetic movement, only double
down on their grandiose claims and their "great swelling words."

The reader may well be asking, what is the relevance of this
to the IHOP movement of today? The answer is that Mike Bickle
considers the emergence of the Kansas City Prophets as part and
parcel of the prophetic history of IHOP. "The Prophetic History
of IHOP" is the subject of a series of teachings Bickle offers on
his website, titled "Encountering Jesus: Visions, Revelations, and
Angelic Activity from IHOPKC's Prophetic History."

> Over the last 25 plus years, the Lord has graciously
> given us about 25 powerful prophetic experiences
> that provide insight into what will happen in the days
> ahead in Kansas City, the USA, and other nations.
> These supernatural experiences were given to several
> prophetic people in the 1970s and 1980s. They include
> times when various believers saw the Lord, heard God's
> audible voice, saw an angel, or had prophetic dreams
> that were dramatically confirmed. These prophetic
> experiences are referred to as IHOP-KC's prophetic
> history.[5]

The bizarre and false "prophecies" of Bob Jones and Paul Cain are considered to be valid and foundational to the IHOP movement. It becomes obvious to the listener or reader of Bickle's history of the movement, that he hasn't repudiated the teachings and prophecies of these disgraced prophets.

I wouldn't send anyone to IHOP because there have been too many reports coming out of it of cultic tendencies . . .

No wonder so many who have actually experienced IHOP come away with cult-like reports of heavy shepherding, misuse of prophecy, and other sociologically cultish tendencies.

Here are some examples of testimonies to this assertion.

From a Grieving Father

I'VE LOST A SON to a thing called IHOP—he told me that "older and wiser council" had met with him. It was, therefore, his decision (after meeting with this "older and wiser counsel") that he and I should have ZERO communication for "one year . . . at least."

That's the beginning of a great novel in the making. It's also the sad, sad truth behind the last 2 years and 3 months of my life. The International House of "Prayer" (and unaccredited university) has been the catalyst in tearing a once loving relationship between mother and son in half. But that's not what's caused me to go into such deep mourning . . . [6]

Here is an excerpt from a devastating article called "Why I Believe IHOP is a Cult" from the blog of a longtime student and intern at IHOP.

> A destructive cult's leader is a self-appointed messianic person claiming to have a special mission in life. For example, leaders of flying saucer cults claim that beings from outer space have commissioned them to lead people away from Earth, so that only the leaders can save them from impending doom.

Every intern was required to listen to the 12 hours of IHOP's recorded history on CD footage. Much of this content was heavily edited before its publication. These tapes told of "prophetic words" and signs that were given to some of Mike's mentors (Bob Jones, Paul Cain, etc)—who were all naming him as the leader of the next "big thing" God was doing. Over and over and over again I've heard it said (both directly by Mike as well as from others) that he (Mike) would be the leader of a movement that "changed the nature and expression of Christianity in the earth." Every time, all recognition points to Mike. His "mission" to transform the church and capture the hearts of America's youth has been his declared goal since the early 1980's. One of the major dangers is that these grandious sounding claims and "prophetic" words are laden with flattery, narcissism, elitism and are a perfect guise under which anything Mike introduces through IHOP can fall under the heading of being a "new thing" God is doing.

This elitist teaching puts Mike on a pedestal and he has a Messianic-like devoted following of people who would do anything if he told them to without a moment of questioning or hesitation. From my observations and experiences on staff, IHOP members do not think for themselves or question Mike's interpretation of scripture or the slant in the way he teaches it. At any conference, one will easily observe that if Mike recommends a book or promotes a teaching, a t-shirt or a speaker, at the next break, ALL of that item will be sold out in their bookstore. When I was on staff, I heard people continually sing Mike's praises around the clock and quote more of what Mike says or thinks or teaches than actual scripture.

Mike has an alluring charisma and many seem to be instantly drawn to his convincing appearance of direction and purpose. He teaches with passion and emotion rather than truth and it's that charisma that draws and hooks people causing many to blindly follow (and defend) his message.[7]

The anonymous author at Gospel Masquerade makes a good point, that the twelve plus hours of teaching CDs, the so-called "Prophetic History" of IHOP, (which is required listening to all interns), are full of prophecies and stories which make grandiose claims concerning Bickle and IHOP.

To a certain kind of naive and unwary young constituency it is flattering to believe that Bickle and IHOP are perhaps the greatest movement the world has ever seen, and they are a part of something so powerful!

The effect is cultic in its binding power; who would want to ever leave the "greatest revival movement the world has ever known," or abandon the man (Bickle) who was willing to do what all others approached by the Spirit refused to do? The 12 hours are subjective testimonies, "prophecies," stories, coincidences, and anecdotes, all centered around Bickle, the movement, and the adventures of various (false) prophets, especially Bob Jones.

Consider the spiritual climate generated by the accumulation of the students and interns steeped in these subjective teachings and experienced based spirituality. Most of these students are young people, narcissistic and willing to give all for the greater cause. This is a dangerous mix.

IHOP and The Sensual "Bridal Paradigm"

I WOULD NEVER SEND young people to IHOP because I believe the 'Bridal Paradigm is unbalanced and sensual . . .

We who know the Word of God, all agree that the church is the "Bride of Christ" whom He purchased for Himself with His own blood. There are other metaphors for the church—it is the "household of God" and the "body of the Messiah." It is also the temple of God, and the Army of the Lord, and yes indeed, it is the Bride.

But when the Bridal Paradigm becomes virtually the only one that is emphasized, and when it is forced into something more than the apostles ever would have done, we have a problem.

What happens when people individualize the Bridal Paradigm, and introduce into their worship an erotic element?

Keith Gibson of the Apologetics Research Center summarizes this emphasis:

> God is described as "in love," lovesick, the passionate Bridegroom, or having a ravished heart. He is the Lover with fire in His eyes for His bride. The church is to respond in similar manner as we pray for our love to be awakened, to be ravished by the love of the Bridegroom etc. etc. Images and language from Song of Solomon abound.
>
> This teaching, while drawing upon a legitimate metaphor and the language of Scripture, pushes the metaphor beyond the boundaries of its proper understanding leading to an improper and unbiblical picture of God and His relationship to the Church.[8]

This distortion of a perfectly beautiful New Testament truth has happened before, for example the Roman Catholic mystics would often speak of being "ravished" by Jesus, at times relating their ecstatic experiences into a sensual and erotic realm. It could never truly be said of any individual Christian that they are the "Bride of Christ."

But some of the modern "worship lyricists" are going there, unfortunately, due to this misguided emphasis. John Mark Macmillan, in the song "How He Loves" touches on this in the lyrics:

> We are His portion and He is our prize,

Drawn to redemption by the grace in His eyes,
If grace is an ocean, we're all sinking.
So Heaven meets earth like a sloppy wet kiss,
And the heart turns violently inside of my chest,
I don't have time to maintain this regrets,
When I think about, the way He loves us,
Oh how He loves us.[9]

Perhaps more obvious would be the mass wedding, at the Kansas City Convention Center, as reported by CBN reporter Wendy Griffith, on January 6, 2002.

Some 20,000 mostly young people packed the Kansas City Convention Center on New Year's Eve for a wedding ceremony unlike any other . . . as each person who came embarked on a marriage covenant with the Bridegroom of Heaven . . . From noon until midnight they danced and sang, fasted and prayed, and got ready to get married to Jesus.

"There's going to be a wedding and God is raising up friends of the Bridegroom to prepare the church, there's going to be a wedding!"

One by one, thousands of men and women, young and old, made their vows and walked under the prayer shawl symbolizing their commitment to Jesus . . .

Here is an excerpt from a booklet produced by IHOP which was at one time considered required reading—

He [God] has given Himself to both the exhilarations and the woundings of a lovesick heart. When He gazes upon me, He sees through the eyes of love and desire. He comes before me and says, "I am a Man in love. I am a God that burns with desire, and I have set

My affections on you. I am an all-consuming fire of love, and you are the inheritance that My Father has promised me. Will you receive My love?"[10]

Here, again from the same book, are the lyrics to a song.

O Gaze Eternal,
How penetrating are Your Fires
Rushing through my darkest places
With the burning streams of Desire
Leaving me naked, purged and bare
. . . Yet embraced . . .

You take hold of my weakest places
And kiss them with Your mercy
Lifting up my low grounds
With your mighty love so holy.[11]

This pseudo spiritual erotic sensuality is rapidly infecting unwary evangelical and Pentecostal churches, leading people astray from the true worship and awe of God, into an experienced based form of ecstasy that is more akin to the pagan religions that Christianity once defeated. I predict that with this idolatry will come much immorality and even worse forms of darkness.

The world was shocked in 2013 when a young intern at IHOP confessed to the murder of another 27 year old intern, Bethany Deaton, the wife of Tyler Deaton, one of the IHOP small group staff members.

According to a *Rolling Stone* report, "Love and Death in the House of Prayer," the self-confessed Harry Potter, Lord of the Rings, and Chronicles of Narnia fan felt right at home at IHOP, as a staff member, and simultaneously leading his own sex based cult, in the vicinity of IHOP University!

I am not saying IHOP caused the death or even sanctioned it. I am merely saying that there is a sick, toxic spiritual atmosphere developed, when you combine the "Love sick Jesus" paradigm, as well as toleration of false prophecy, rehabilitation of known sexual deviants into ministry, combined with an extreme spiritual warfare mentality, all night prayer sessions, and add into the mix thousands of young naïve people eager to give all. Something bad is bound to happen.

When an obvious reprobate like Bob Jones is exalted and praised as a great man of God, (after he is exposed as a pervert who abused the so-called gift of prophecy), you are going to attract thousands of other unbalanced and unstable people just like him. (This is where lunatics like John Crowder and Todd Bentley emerge).

I believe that the "bridal paradigm" is a dangerous doctrinal over emphasis , especially for young people. The terms that ought to alert you that it is infiltrating your church are the use of expressions like "ravished heart"(for God), "Lovesick Bride," "ecstasy," over use of the words "intimacy" and "passion," or use of erotic metaphors.

Did the true apostles of our Lord Jesus speak this way?

Certainly the Catholic mystics through the ages spoke thusly, such as Teresa of Avila and St. John of the Cross. But who would want to have their teens and youth influenced by Catholic mystics? Roman Catholic mysticism is not the same as Christian spirituality. It is nearer to Eastern religion, and in some cases (Padre Pio) it leads into the occult. There is a reason Thomas Merton and others became Roman Catholic/Buddhist monks! This brings me to my next objection.

IHOP and Contemplative Prayer

FINALLY I WOULD AVOID IHOP like the plague because Bickle and the IHOP are strong advocates of contemplative prayer, an ancient mystical belief system, with roots in panentheism and occultism.

At IHOP these contemplative "ancient practices" are cherished. John Lanagan, a former New Ager who has researched IHOP extensively, explains:

> Much of the literature being sold through the International House of Prayer's online FORERUNNER Bookstore indicates a contemplative influence. One such book being offered is *Fire Within,* written by Father Thomas Dubay. IHOP founder Mike Bickle states, "I want this book to be the manual for IHOP-KC."
>
> That is high praise for this book from Mike Bickle. The full title of the book is *Fire Within: St. Teresa of Avila, St. John of the Cross, and the Gospel–On Prayer.* [12]

In a video talk given by Mike Bickle in 2008 titled "Fellowshipping with the Holy Spirit: 5 Practical Phrases," Bickle gives instructions on contemplative prayer practices.[13] Lanagan explains:

> Like all Christian contemplatives, Bickle works hard at presenting this as biblically acceptable. He states there is ". . . a lot of counterfeit mysticism . . ." Before teaching his Christianese mantra method, he again emphasizes he is not talking about Eastern or Oprah religion.[14]

In the video, Bickle states:

> I use sentences, better yet phrases. Eventually on these five phrases I'm gonna give you in a minute, I reduce those to one word.[15]

The idea behind contemplative prayer is to take a small phrase or single word, repeat it for several minutes, which is supposed to help the mind "center" or forget all distractions. The practioner experiences a kind of mental detachment going into an altered state of what is called "silence." The contemplative believes that once he is able to get his mind free of all distractions, he will be able to hear the voice of God.

To fully understand the dangers of contemplative prayer, I would suggest you read Ray Yungen's book *A Time of Departing*, which gives a detailed analysis of the origin of contemplative prayer as well as the dangers of practicing contemplative prayer. Yungen shows that the contemplative silence is the same mystical state experienced by occultists as well as practictioners of Eastern meditation and the New Age.

Mike Bickle is clearly an open advocate of contemplative prayer as are many of the figures in this modern-day prophets and apostles movement. Bickle believes it is something precious that has been restored back to the church. In an audio message, Mike Bickle states:

> The Protestant wing of the western church, which is a tiny percentage of the Body of Christ . . . is nearly completely (98%) unaware that the Holy Spirit is restoring contemplative prayer—center stage—to the church . . . The Holy Spirit is restoring this precious jewel (contemplative prayer) to the body of Christ. This is the God ordained means of attaining the fullness of God."[16]

Extreme mental passivity, visualization and self-hypnosis by use of a mantra are all methods employed by the heathen to enter into (non-Christian) spiritual experiences. We must remember that any spirituality that is not biblical is demonic. The Bible is clear in both Testaments:

> But I say, that the things which the Gentiles sacrifice, they sacrifice to devils, and not to God: and I would not that ye should have fellowship with devils.(1

Corinthians 10:20)

And they shall no more offer their sacrifices unto
devils, after whom they have gone a whoring. This
shall be a statute for ever unto them throughout their
generations.(Leviticus 17:7)

Wherever there is false prophecy allowed, sooner or later,
there will be immorality and the occult. It's inevitable. Roman
Catholic mysticism, centering prayer, contemplative prayer,
dream interpretation, personal prophecy, are all just varying
degrees of departure from the Truth.

All of these reasons that I have laid forth in this chapter
show that IHOP is a dangerous and spiritually toxic movement.

7

Todd Bentley—A Disaster in Discernment and Morality

ONE OF THE MORE flamboyant evangelists operating in "prophetic" circles is Todd Bentley. The story of his rise to prominence, his endorsement by apostolic and prophetic leadership, the failure of his marriage and his subsequent "restoration" are proof positive to any "who have ears to hear" that this whole movement is an utter sham.

Bentley comes from a little town in British Columbia, on Canada's western coast. He was early involved in drugs, alcohol, and as a juvenile, was convicted of the sexual abuse of a younger boy. After experiencing several drug overdoses, Bentley eventually underwent a Christian conversion at the age of 19.

Shortly after this conversion, Bentley began his ministry, evangelizing and giving his testimony at churches and in special revival meetings. In 1998, Bentley gave his testimony at a group called Fresh Fire Ministry. In a short time, he was asked to lead the group, which became known as an "international revival" group. He came into notoriety when Stephan Strader, pastor of Ignited Church of Lakeland, Florida asked him to do a series of revival meetings.

Through a combination of savvy marketing on the Internet, (the early services were broadcast on Ustream, receiving over a million hits within the first five weeks) and the eventual full coverage by "GOD TV" (a European Christian television network), the "Lakeland Revival" became a widely known phenomenon.

Todd Bentley's appearance and manner are often shocking to those first exposed to him. He is covered with tattoos,(something he says God told him to do, since becoming an evangelist). This is disturbing, because the tattoos Todd sports feature images of false gods, occult symbols, flames, and body piercing. It is almost as if he is daring people to judge him based on "outward appearance."

Todd is the embodiment of a rebellious and perhaps idolatrous ideal among Pentecostals and some evangelicals—the "outlaw" preacher. A kind of Christianized "rebel without a cause," who is (supposedly) more genuine than the more formal "suit and tie" preachers of old.

Of course it is true that God judges not by outward appearance, but how far should we take that? Does that mean that an evangelist should cover himself with tattoos and piercings of demonic and occult symbols, so that he can dare (normal) people to judge him? Should we all dress as provocatively as possible to make this point?

Bentley also disparages formal training in theology and doctrine, and postures as the back woods biker, uneducated person, who unlike the theologian, truly has the goods, having experienced God directly through his many visions, dreams, revelations and visitations.

Evidently tens of thousands of God's people love to have it so, for they poured into the "Lakeland Revival" in the thousands, and eagerly tuned into GOD TV's full revival coverage to revel in the outrageous and even blasphemous antics of Todd Bentley.

What did they tune into?

They came to see and experience Bentley's unorthodox "healing methods." Bentley claimed in a service that when he asked the Lord why revival hadn't come yet to the church, Bentley's visionary Jesus told him it was because he hadn't "punched an older man in the stomach yet." Irish Central News reports in an article explaining why Bentley was literally banned from the UK, that Bentley says the Holy Spirit told him to kick a sweet old lady worshipping the Lord in the face!

In videos, he is heard telling audiences, "And the Holy Spirit spoke to me, the gift of faith came on me. He said, 'kick her in the face with your biker boot.' I inched closer and I went like this—bam! And just as my boot made contact with her nose, she fell under the power of God."[1]

I have seen Bentley punch a person in the stomach, doubling him up in obvious pain. Bentley had first inquired what the man's condition was and was told "Stage 4 stomach Cancer." Bentley's assurance to the man he struck, "Sometimes when you are being healed it gets worse before it gets better."

I suppose a lot of the thousands also come to hear Bentley's preaching. Bentley's doctrine is Manifested Sons of God, Kingdom Dominion, Faith Message teaching mixed in with the neo-Gnostic personal revelations Bentley has acquired. On his chest is tattooed "Joel's Army," a misinterpretation of the true prophet Joel's vision as taught by the false prophet Paul Cain.

Bentley rarely even attempts to expound the Word of God, for most of his preaching consists of a series of outlandish stories and testimonies of various healings Bentley and others have performed and even a few resurrections (twenty to date). He also entices the crowds with stories of his own personal mystical experiences; fire tunnels, whirlwinds, angelic appearances, revelations, prophecies, miracles and healings.

In other words, as the prophet Jeremiah said:

> I have heard what the prophets say who prophesy lies in my name. They say, "I had a dream! I had a dream!" How long will this continue in the hearts of these lying prophets, who prophesy the delusions of their own minds? They think the dreams they tell one another will make my people forget my name, just as their ancestors forgot my name through Baal worship. Let the prophet who has a dream recount the dream, but let the one who

has my word speak it faithfully. For what has straw to do with grain?" declares the Lord. "Is not my word like fire," declares the Lord, "and like a hammer that breaks a rock in pieces? . . ." (Jeremiah 23:25-29)

Why do God's people prefer straw to grain?

An Immoral Commissioning

IN JUNE OF 2008, ten of the "Apostles and Prophets" of the NAR held an internationally televised commissioning service for Bentley, laying hands on him and prophesying over him in the name of the Lord. *Charisma* described the event:

> California pastors Ché Ahn and Bill Johnson, along with Canadian pastor John Arnott [pastor of the Toronto Airport Vineyard—now called Catch the Fire] laid hands on the 32-year-old Bentley while Peter Wagner, leader of the International Coalition of Apostles, read a statement about the need for apostolic alignment. Other prominent leaders from the apostolic and prophetic movements stood on the platform to show their support for Bentley and to endorse the revival, which began in early April and is now in its 83rd day of continuous meetings.

> The ceremony, held in a 10,000-seat tent, took place after some charismatic leaders raised questions about Bentley's claims, methods and theology. They asked Wagner to oversee a dialogue, and he responded by organizing Monday evening's event so that Bentley could have more accountability—or what Wagner calls "apostolic alignment." . . .

> Participating leaders at the ceremony included Wagner; Ché Ahn, pastor of Harvest Rock Church in Pasadena, Calif.; John Arnott of Toronto Airport Christian

Fellowship in Canada; Bill Johnson, pastor of Bethel Church in Redding, Calif.; and Rick Joyner, founder of MorningStar Ministries in Charlotte, N.C.[2]

This commissioning service came at a time when there were valid and well-founded concerns being expressed by some regarding Todd Bentley's methods, theology, and claims. Instead of these so-called apostles investigating these concerns to see if there was a legitimate problem, they organized this public "commissioning" of Bentley.

The "prophetic words" spoken by these men can only truly be described in the manner Peter and Jude foretold as "great swelling words of vanity . . . having men's persons in admiration."

Here is an example of this from the "commissioning service," a "Word" over Bentley by "Presiding Apostle" C. Peter Wagner:

> This commissioning represents a powerful spiritual transaction taking place in the invisible world. With this in mind, I take the apostolic authority that God has given me and I decree to Todd Bentley, your power will increase, your authority will increase, your favor will increase, your influence will increase, your revelation will increase.
>
> I also decree that a new supernatural strength will flow through this ministry. A new life force will penetrate this move of God. Government will be established to set things in their proper order. God will pour out a higher level of discernment to distinguish truth from error. New relationships will surface to open the gates to the future.[3]

All of this was widely celebrated and agreed upon throughout the charismatic prophetic community. Bentley himself was duly impressed by the powerful words spoken over him as expressed in the following:

I am no church historian, but I do not know of any
other time in history, since the book of Acts, have so
many different apostles and so many different prophets
and movements and leaders [been represented]," Bentley
said of the capacity crowd. "This is so much bigger than
[anything else] ever before. The devil is shaking in his
boots because the apostles are gathering and the prophets
are gathering.[4]

The events which would unfold within days of this public spec-
tacle would serve as a revelation of the utter spiritual bankruptcy
of this self-proclaimed prophetic movement.

Of his commissioning by this *cream of the crop* group of
apostles and prophets, Bentley stated:

"I believe last night was truly historic and a true sign
of unity," Bentley told *Charisma* today. "Many streams
converged and I know last night's commissioning will
truly help bring God's outpouring to a much larger
part of the body." Participating leaders at the ceremony
included Wagner; Ahn, pastor of Harvest Rock Church
in Pasadena, Calif.; John Arnott of Toronto Airport
Christian Fellowship in Canada; Bill Johnson, pastor
of Bethel Church in Redding, Calif.; and Rick Joyner,
founder of MorningStar Ministries in Charlotte, N.C.[5]

As these prophets pontificated over the bright future of Bentley,
it would be less than a year later that Bentley would abandon his
own wife and children and pursue a relationship with his children's
nanny, and in fact, he was already involved with this other woman
when the commissing service too place.

Religion News Service wrote this in March 2009 in an article
titled "Controversial 'evangelist' Todd Bentley marries woman he
had extramarital affair with."

> [Todd] Bentley has married the former Jessa Hasbrook, a former intern for his ministry. Last summer, his internationally famous revival campaign in Lakeland, Florida collapsed when it was revealed that he and Jessa had begun an "emotional affair." Charismatic leaders C. Peter Wagner and Robert Ricciardelli, however, have reported that the affair was apparently sexual. Mr. Ricciardelli, furthermore, has indicated that this affair, whatever type it was, began in January of last year, which would place it well before Mr. Bentley announced that he was separating from his wife Shonnah. This is also well before Mr. Bentley brought Shonnah Bentley and his kids to Lakeland to show them to an international T.V. audience. Shonnah Bentley even preached in a local church to promote her husband's revival.

Try to take in the implications of this stunning betrayal by Bentley. He knew already that he was committing adultery but commenced the Lakeland meetings anyway. At one point, he allowed his wife and children to publically promote him, even parading them on television, knowing he was preparing to leave them.

How is it that these men of such "intimacy" with God who had received such grandiose visions and words for Todd couldn't perceive what even an unsaved person with common sense could have told them?

What do you do when a false prophet you have been following and exalting has been exposed as a fraud, a liar, and an adulterer?

Repentance is called for, for the implications of following false prophets are extensive.

But among those who stood in the name of God anointing a charlatan, there was no such repentance. Incredibly, their concern seemed to be how to get Bentley back into public ministry as quickly as possible!

Charisma editor J. Lee Grady spoke the truth in his March 2009 editorial "The Tragic Scandal of Greasy Grace":

What is most deplorable about this latest installment in the Bentley scandal is the lack of true remorse. In his own statement, Bentley apologizes for his actions and says he "takes full responsibility for my part for the ending of the marriage." But how can he be taking "full responsibility" if he willingly chose to have a girlfriend on the side—and then married her immediately after his divorce was final? Why did he hide for several months when he should have been listening to counsel and seeking reconciliation with his first wife?

Grady decried the rush to restore Bentley to ministry, the insistence by those who stood on that stage that the Lakeland Revival was valid, the strange lack of any concern whatsoever of Shonnah, Bentley's wounded ex-wife, and of his three children, and the overall lack of concern for the name of Christ!

In all the discussion of Bentley and the demise of the Lakeland Revival, I am waiting to hear the sound of sackcloth ripping into shreds. We should be weeping. We should be rending our hearts—as God commanded Israel when they fell into sin (see Joel 2: 13-14). To give guidance to a confused church, our leaders should have publicly decried the Lakeland disaster while at the same time helping both Todd and Shonnah to heal.

But where are those apostles and prophets mourning this travesty? Are they shocked and appalled that such sin has been named among them. Or do they behave as if flippant divorce and remarriage are minor infractions—when in actuality they are such serious moral failures that they can bring disqualification?[6]

There was of course a statement by Bentley, after the fact, asking for forgiveness, and assuring the body of Christ that he was doing better now, healing and resting

from the Lakeland outpouring, and that he had come
under the restoration process through the ministry of
Bill Johnson, Rick Joyner, and Jack Deere. See more at:
http://www.god.tv/news/rick-joyner-interviewed-about-
todd-bentley#sthash.m08deZBN.dpuf

Bentley's "restoration" to "ministry" came in increments. His
overseers wanted him to be able to minister in "safe places" where
he could be monitored, so MorningStar ministries allowed Todd to
minister there with his new wife. Eventually he was allowed to minister on the Internet "training leaders" to walk in the supernatural.

By May 2010, Rick Joyner pronounced Bentley to be completely restored and ready for limited local ministry. By 2011,
Bentley was "released" to go international with his new wife
prophesying alongside him.

Bentley's Propensity for Contemplative Mysticism

THE FOLLOWING INFORMATION WILL show Bentley's spiritual res-
onance with a man named Sundar Singh (1829-1929). At one
point in Bentley's ministry, he had a vision of Sundar Singh – this
vision greatly influenced Bentley. According to a biographer of
Sundar Singh, Singh spent much of his Christian life in deep
trance-like states communicating with spiritual beings.

> We know he had long hours of meditation . . . Also he
> had days of silence. . . . One day . . . he was in the woods
> praying. . . . Suddenly his spiritual eyes were opened and
> he saw the glories of the spirit world. After that he had
> visions from time to time. Later on the visions came as
> often as ten or twelve times a month and he then had
> long talks with the beings of that world.[7]

One of those "beings" identified himself as Emmanuel Swedenborg, an occult visionary who had lived 150 years before Singh.
As the deceased "Emmanuel Swedenborg" appeared to Singh and

communicated with him, the deceased "Singh" communicated to Bentley in his (Todd Bentley's) vision:

> I saw in a vision, the Glory Cloud of Revelation descending upon the church. It was also during this time of prayer that God took me in a vision to what I believed to be the Himalayan Mountains. I saw an Indian man with a turban on his head and heard the whisper of the Spirit say, "This is Sundar Singh. I am releasing anointing of revelation like this." I had no communication with this old saint, nor did he say anything to me. The experience lasted only a moment. . . .[8]

Why would God give his children a vision of a contemplative who combined the East and West in his meditative disciplines? Is this where Todd Bentley's ideas about visions, spirituality, and "soaking" prayer are coming from?

The simple answer is that Todd Bentley has gone beyond heretical Christianity, and even false prophecy. He is into the occult. He is a necromancer, one who communicates with the dead. He teaches other his techniques as well.

There is a Todd Bentley resource CD called "Developing Your Seer Gift." Some of the ways in which Todd Bentley teaches to develop your inner seer gift is by "Activating Your Spiritual Senses" and by opening "Spiritual Gates, Doors and Portals."

> There are over eight ways that Todd will outline in this teaching that will help you position yourself for God to open the eyes of your heart, such as: overcoming fear of the unknown, meditating in your heart and being still, soaking and contemplative prayer, and meditating on God's Word.
>
> ...Todd will give clarification, both through the Word of God and by sharing amazing personal experiences, how

spiritual gates, doors and portals trigger supernatural encounters with God. Using Jacob's life as an example, Todd will teach you how to position yourself for a holy visitation from God.[9]

The Bible warns us about spiritual realms and principalities. Rather than teaching about contemplative spirituality and opening the gates to the dangers of the supernatural, a real shepherd would be more concerned about laying down his life to protect his sheep.

A wonderful and horrible thing is committed in the land;
The prophets prophesy falsely,
and the priests bear rule by their means;
and my people love to have it so:
and what will ye do in the end thereof?
(Jeremiah 5:31)

8

Bill Johnson—Experience-Based Christianity

WHAT WOULD YOU THINK of a Bible school that sends young people out to literally prostrate themselves on the graves of deceased preachers so that the students can absorb "the anointing" that lingers on the graves? What about a church in which a mist containing feathers, gold, and jewel dust descends on the worshippers in the sanctuary? How about a church conference which features prophetic "tattoo readings" as one of the workshops?

What would you expect of a church which is a combination of the Word of Faith error and the prosperity gospel of Kenneth Copeland and Kenneth Hagin, the signs and wonders of Oral Roberts and Benny Hinn, the false assumptions of the spiritual warfare and hyper-deliverance movement, the "prophetic movement" I have been describing in this book, and the gnostic mysticism of the Toronto Blessing?

You don't have to wonder any longer for there is such a "ministry" which is currently the most recognizable and influential face of the prophetic movement. I refer to Bill and Beni Johnson who co-pastor Bethel Assembly of Redding California and its related ministries, including "Jesus Culture" youth band and Bethel's School of Supernatural Ministry.

Bill Johnson, a noted conference speaker and leader, is the author of several best-selling books and considered to be an apostle and leader within the Apostles and Prophets movement. Hundreds of thousands have been affected by his ministry and have attended retreats and conferences where they have been "imparted" with "the anointing."

In order to fully understand the prophetic movement in its current state, we must examine the teachings and ministry of Bill Johnson in the light of the Word of God. Didn't Jesus warn us not to be naïve but that "every tree is known by its fruits"?

> Beware of false prophets, which come to you in sheep's clothing, but inwardly they are ravening wolves. Ye shall know them by their fruits. Do men gather grapes of thorns, or figs of thistles? Even so every good tree bringeth forth good fruit; but a corrupt tree bringeth forth evil fruit. A good tree cannot bring forth evil fruit, neither can a corrupt tree bring forth good fruit.Every tree that bringeth not forth good fruit is hewn down, and cast into the fire. Wherefore by their fruits ye shall know them.(Matthew7:15-20)

The primary "fruit" of any professed prophet would be the teaching. (The same would go for any pastor or apostle or anyone who stands in the name of God).

Let's examine some of Bill Johnson's teachings.

The Word of Faith Movement

IT DOESN'T TAKE LONG to see by reading his books that Johnson is a proponent of the Word of Faith teaching, popularized by Kenneth Hagin and Kenneth Copeland. Therefore, it is necessary to give a brief overview of WOF teaching to be able to see where Johnson is coming from.

In a nutshell, the WOF teaching is based on a gnostic interpretation of the Fall and of redemption. The following is their explanation:

When God created Adam, He gave him all dominion over the earth, to rule and reign as God's regent. However when Adam fell, by obeying Satan, he handed that God-given dominion over to Satan, who became the "god of this world." God, the Father, couldn't just come in and take the dominion back—Adam had given it away.

God had to find a way for a man to come in, as a man, and undo the folly of Adam, gaining back the authority given to Satan by Adam. Jesus is that man. (The WOF teachers do acknowledge that Jesus is God but believe that He "laid aside His own Divinity" in the Incarnation).

As a man, Jesus came into the world, resisted all of the temptation that Adam and Eve and the human race succumbed to, and died on the Cross as a sacrifice for our sins.

But there is a twist, for the WOF teachers insist that salvation wasn't secured for man in Jesus' death on the Cross as a substitute for our sins. Rather, Jesus first had to descend into hell and suffer the torment of Satan and his minions until God was satisfied that it was enough and could *legally* raise Him from the dead.

Of course, the Word of God says that Jesus' death on the Cross was sufficient, and that when He said, "Telestai!" (It is done), it really was done. But Copeland and Hagin teach that it wasn't finished until Jesus had literally "become sin" and endured demonic torment in hell.

The fall, according to WOF, was as much about the loss of power and authority as it was about sin and alienation from God. Therefore salvation is about restoration of power and authority, as well as forgiveness of sins. We get the power back and can now exercise dominion over this life and take authority over evil.

Because of this skewed view, WOF is a power religion. This is why WOF Christians frequently speak in terms of authority; they "bind and/or loose" angels and demons; they decree, rebuke, and otherwise speak in terms of "releasing" peace, grace, or mercy into this situation or that.

The essence of this theology is the restoration and practical use of the "authority to the believer."

The ideal in WOF circles is that of the born again man of power and authority, the miracle man who has come in to the "revelation knowledge" of "who he is in Christ," and demonstrates the power of "the anointing" to a lost world. There have developed extensive mythologies around truly historical figures such as Smith Wigglesworth, John Alexander Dowie, John G. Lake, and William Branham. These are the men who really "took authority," they say, and showed us all what any believer could do, if they have but the faith and "anointing" to do so!

The WOF is an offshoot of an earlier expression of these very ideals, the Manifested Sons of God, once repudiated by the Assemblies of God in the 1940s but now widely embraced in this new form. MSG is based upon an erroneous interpretation of Romans 8:19, "For the earnest expectation of the creature waiteth for the manifestation of the sons of God."

Traditional Christianity has held that this verse refers to what happens at the bodily coming of the Lord. When Jesus returns, the curse on Creation will finally be removed, and the true children of God will be manifested.

But the MSG teach that this verse means that the Creation is waiting for the church to attain to the knowledge of the power and authority, in order to "manifest" our Sonship to the world, through signs and wonders. All of this must occur before Jesus can come back!

This is the context in which to understand where Bill Johnson, Jesus Culture, and the Bethel School of Supernatural Ministry are coming from, as they seek to bring the church into the power and anointing of their "mystical revival."

Three of Bill Johnson's Teachings

JOHNSON'S TEACHING GOES ERRANT on so many levels that it is hard to decide where to begin. For the sake of brevity, I will address three areas of concern: a) Johnson's teachings on the Incarnation; b) the anointing (Holy Ghost); and c) and his theology of experience. I urge you to be the judge according to the test in Deuteronomy 13.

In his teaching on the Incarnation, Bill Johnson states, and rightly so, that Jesus Christ is God. But Johnson also emphasizes to an unbiblical extreme that Jesus completely laid aside His deity:

> Jesus had no ability to heal the sick. He couldn't cast out devils, and He had no ability to raise the dead. He said of Himself in John 5:19, "the Son can do nothing of Himself." He had set aside His divinity. He did miracles as man in right relationship with God because He was setting forth a model for us, something for us to follow. If He did miracles as God, we would all be extremely impressed, but we would have no compulsion to emulate Him. But when we see that God has commissioned us to do what Jesus did- and more- Then we realize that He put self-imposed restrictions on Himself to show us that we could do it, too. Jesus so emptied Himself that He was incapable of doing what was required of Him by The Father-without the Father's help.[1]

There are several problems with this teaching of Johnson's. For example, it is theologically inaccurate to say that "Jesus had no ability . . ." and that Jesus "set aside His Divinity." It is dangerously close to being a denial of the Deity of Christ, for divinity by definition cannot be "set aside" nor could God ever be said to lack ability in any sense.

In the Incarnation, the eternal God became a man, though He never ceased being God. He always had all power, but restrained Himself, declining the prerogatives of power and majesty, which are inherent to Him, that He might live and die for us as true man.

Another problem with this is that Johnson asserts that Jesus performed miracles to "set forth a model for us . . . to show us that we could do it (the miracles) too . . ."

This is at the very heart of the Word of Faith teaching from which Johnson has emerged. Supposedly, we as individual believers, can and should be doing all of the miracles of Jesus, in the power of the Spirit. To Johnson, Jesus came in the flesh, partly to show us, that we too could do what He did!

This quest for miracle power is misguided and has led many into deception. Jesus didn't do His miracles to "show us that we can do it." The miracles of Jesus are manifestations of the merciful God, whether they be the ones in the Gospels, or in the Book of Acts, or those done in His name throughout the world today. "These signs will follow those that believe." We are not to seek them. It is only a "wicked and adulterous generation (which) seeks after signs."

Johnson actually posits that any believer has the potential to experience most of what Jesus experienced in the Gospels, even the Transfiguration! He states:

> Most all of the experiences of Jesus recorded in Scripture were prophetic examples of the realms in God that are made available to the believer. The Mount of Transfiguration raised the bar significantly on potential human experience…The overwhelming lesson in this story is that Jesus Christ, the Son of man, had the glory of God upon Him. Jesus's face shone with God's glory, similar to Moses's after he came down from the mountain.[2]

Johnson seems to fail to appreciate that though Jesus became "as one of us" in the Incarnation, His uniqueness cannot be safely diminished. Imagine a spirituality spent seeking to attain a transfiguration! No wonder Johnson's students go to such lengths seeking "glory" experiences.

The second aspect of Johnson's teaching that is dangerous and has led to the reckless mysticism in which so many associated with Bethel are involved is what he teaches about the Holy Spirit, particularly "the anointing." Johnson states:

> Christ is not Jesus' last name. The word Christ means
> "Anointed One" or "Messiah . . . [Christ] is a title that
> points to an experience. It was not sufficient that Jesus
> be sent from heaven to earth with a title. He had to
> receive the anointing in an experience to accomplish
> what the Father desired.[3]

First of all, here is an example of a teacher setting forth an
unbiblical separation between the person "Jesus" and the word
"Christ." This is a very dangerous thing to do; it is similar to what
the New Age movement claims, and it is being done towards a
similar end.

New Agers want to establish the (false) idea that Jesus was
merely an enlightened person, one who was anointed (Christed)
at thirty years old, very similar to other remarkable human beings
such as Ghandi and Zoroaster. This "anointing" is a self-realizing
experience.

Johnson seems to be trying to establish that just as the man
Jesus had to be anointed with the Holy Ghost in order (as a man)
to do the miracles He did, we too can have the same experience
to do the same thing, for Jesus is our model.

The Bible doesn't do this with the word "Christ." The apostles
never relegated Christ as being a title, nor as being an experience.
Christ is a designation of Jesus' deity. Scripture insists that Jesus
is the Christ, and it refers to Jesus as Christ, "God was in Christ
reconciling the world unto himself. . ." Christ is an eternal person,
chosen of God, thus anointed with the Holy Ghost.

When Jesus came into the world, He already *was* Christ; he
never had to become Christ.

On the same subject—the "anointing"—Johnson continues:

> The word anointing means "to smear." The Holy Spirit
> is the oil of God that was smeared all over Jesus at His
> water baptism. The name Jesus Christ implies that Jesus
> is the One smeared with the Holy Spirit.

> The outpouring of the Spirit also needed to happen to Jesus for Him to be fully qualified. This was His quest. Receiving this anointing qualified Him to be called the Christ, which means "anointed one." Without the experience [the anointing] there could be no title.[4]

Do you see the problems Johnson's teachings on "the anointing" raise?

For example, did Jesus become the Christ at His baptism? If "Christ" is only valid upon an experience, what was Jesus before the Holy Ghost came upon Him in the Jordan? Was He merely an unqualified "man with a title" up until then?

Johnson's view on the Christ is strikingly reminiscent of an error which emerged early in the history of the church and was repudiated as heresy. It is called *adoptionism*. It holds that Jesus was a devout man who did not become "Christed" until He was thirty years old when He was anointed of the Holy Ghost. It was by the Holy Ghost that He did His miracles, but the "anointing" left Him when He died on the Cross. If Jesus could do these things (through revelation knowledge and the anointing), so could any other believer.

There is a passage in 1 John 5 that refutes this very error about the Christ:

> This is he that came by water and blood, even Jesus Christ; not by water only, but by water and blood. And it is the Spirit that beareth witness, because the Spirit is truth.(1 John 5:6)

The heretics were teaching that Jesus was not Christ until He was baptized in water and anointed with the Spirit. He remained Christ until He shed His blood. But the apostle insists that "He came by water and blood;" that is, He was already Christ when He was baptized and remained so on the Cross, and through His resurrection. The designation, "Christ," was and is more than an experience; it is inherent to Jesus, the Divine God/man.

Finally, Bethel is actually dangerous in its approach to doctrine and experience.

What is it in the teachings that has opened those exposed to it, to such practices as:

- False Prophecy?
- Visualization?
- "Fire Tunnels"?
- Grave Soaking trips?[5]
- Visualization, contemplative prayer and meditation practices?
- Chanting, Soaking, and Spiritual Drunkenness?
- "Toking" the Holy Ghost to get High on Jesus?

In addition to "normal" prophetic words, those who attended Bethel's "Power and Love Conference" in February 2014 received readings based on their tattoos and piercings. Doug Addison can interpret the hidden messages on your body and even train you to do the same. You don't even have to fly to where he is; for the reasonable fee of $150, he can tickle your ears over the phone for thirty minutes.[6]

Believe me when I say I have just scratched the surface of the irrational, unbiblical, and even anti-biblical practices of Bill Johnson's influential ministry. How do confessing Christians become so open and undiscerning?

There is one aspect of Bethel that is perhaps the most dangerous. Johnson, like so many Pentecostals and evangelicals who have preceded him, has a strong anti-doctrinal emphasis. To the neo-mystics of the New Apostolic Reformation, doctrine has a deadening effect and is valid only to the extent that it induces experience. Doctrine is "the letter which kills," and leads to "head knowledge," as opposed to the personal experience of God, based upon individual revelation.

Those who insist on adherence to true doctrine are caricatured as Pharisees. There are familiar clichés in these circles such as "God is offending the mind to reach the heart," and "a man with an experience is never at the mercy of a man with a doctrine." These kinds of preachers often delight in saying, "I am going to upend your theology now . . ." as they unveil the latest nugget of ther own revelation.

> Jesus made a frightening statement regarding those who hold to Bible Study vs. experience, "You search the Scriptures, for in them you think you have eternal life, and these are they which testify of me" (John 5:39). If our study of the Bible doesn't lead us to a deeper relationship (an encounter) with God, then it is simply adding to our tendency towards spiritual pride. We increase our knowledge of the Bible to feel good about our standing with God, and to better equip us to argue with those who disagree with us. Any group wanting to defend a doctrine is prone to this temptation without a God encounter . . . Jesus did not say 'My sheep will know my Book," it is his voice that we are to know.[7]

Johnson is deconstructing those who seek scriptural knowledge as being in danger of "spiritual pride," increasing in knowledge in order to "feel good about their standing with God," and to be better able to win arguments with those who disagree with them! What a pastor! It is almost as if he would discourage the desire to grow in scriptural knowledge!

But on the other hand, it is the ones seeking "deeper knowledge" (than that which Scripture reveals?) and a deeper encounter with God (experience) whom Johnson considers to be blessed. Imagine a young person sitting under a steady diet of this and you will see why Bethel, Jesus Culture, and the School of Supernatural Ministry are given over to the most sensual mysticism!

9

Prophets and More Prophets

Bill Hamon

We stand at the most crucial crossroads in the history of our nation! We must hear the Word of the Lord that will prepare our way into the next century! The future generations depend on this word! The prophetic streams across this nation are uniting to sound a clear trumpet for the future! This uniting of the streams will form the bedrock for revelation for the River of Revival! Prophets help to prepare the way for the Apostles to establish the Lord's Church.[1]

ONE OF THE MOST prominent and influential of the new prophets is Bill Hamon. As the founder of Christian International Ministries, he has been in the prophetic ministry for over fifty years, and has dedicated much of his ministry to the restoration of the office of the prophet. Hamon is considered by many to be the father of the prophetic movement, and he dedicated his book, *Prophets and Personal Prophecy* to "the great company of prophets God is raising up in these last days." He has been holding prophetic conferences and a school of the prophets for many years now and is considered by those within the movement to be one of the leading prophetic voices of our day. His book sets forth the "theology" of the prophetic movement with such sentiments as:

> The prophets are being brought forth to fulfill their part in preparing the Bride-Church for her day of presentation to her heavenly Bridegroom, Christ Jesus. Jesus is rejoicing with great joy over the part the prophets are playing in preparing his Bride. When the prophets have fininished their ministry, He will be released to descend from heaven with a shout and be fully and eternally united with his Bride. Twentieth-century prophets are very precious to Christ, for they are perfecting the Bride He died to purchase, the church.[2]

As you can see, this is nothing more than the man-centered Manifested Sons of God theology, which has Jesus waiting to be "released" by us, the Last-Days cutting-edge, victorious church! In this case, He awaits the new prophets to perfect His Bride. Hamon states in the same chapter that "Jesus is thrilled at the thought that His prophets will soon be fully recognized and accepted by His Church."

Contrary to what Hamon is stating, the only apostles and prophets that it is essential that the church recognize are the ones who have given us the New Testament. It is the faith "which was once delivered unto the saints" that the church has been founded on, not "twentieth [or twentieth-first] century prophets and apostles." One would get the idea that Jesus is being held back from returning because the church has failed to receive prophets like Rick Joyner, Bob Jones, and Bill Hamon!

The Latter Rain/Manifested Sons of God Theology is flawed in that it often confuses the person of Christ with the Body of Christ, the church. To the church is often assigned the prerogatives and responsibilities that are reserved for Christ alone! It is not the church, but Christ Jesus who will subdue all of God's enemies, including death itself. The hope of the ages is the *parousia*, the actual physical return of Christ Jesus, not the "Great Last Days Revival," or the "Restoration of the new apostles and prophets." The purposes of God are wrapped up in Jesus Christ, and it is in

Him who has come and remains in the flesh. It has never been about man. "I must decrease and He must increase," said "the greatest prophet born of a woman." By the way, that was John the Baptist, not William Branham, Paul Cain, or Bill Hamon.

The new prophets dream of a day of dazzling worldly influence, as can be seen in the following "word":

> The President of the United States and heads of nations will begin to seek out the Christian prophets and prophetic ministers to find out what is really taking place and to know what to do. World conditions will come to the place that human hearts will be failing them for fear. The manipulators that control the economy, stock market, and world banking systems will lose their control. God will cut their puppet strings and take things out of their hands. Only those who know how to hear and speak the true mind of Christ and the Word of God will have the answers. The Joseph and Daniel Prophetic company will arise with the supernatural answers for the needs of the Egyptian Pharaohs, and Babylonian emperors of this world. The prophetic church will finally demonstrate fully that Jesus Christ really is the answer for the world—not only to save them from their sins, but to bring peace on earth and goodwill toward all people.[3]

And there you have it, folks. Two thousand years of biblical instruction proven wrong by the new prophets. Ironic how my Bible says that . . . "ye shall be hated of all men for my name's sake . . . " (Matthew 10:22), and that the apostles who actually knew our Lord, who talked with him face-to-face, ate with Him, touched Him, and witnessed His resurrection and ascension were " . . . made as the filth of the world, and are the offscouring of all things unto this day" (1 Corinthians 4:13). But we are to believe that the new prophets are actually going to be welcomed into the halls of palaces before the world's kings and presidents, who will seek them out to know what God would have them do.

Uh, no.

Jesus warned us repeatedly that:

> If the world hate you, ye know that it hated me before it hated you. If ye were of the world, the world would love his own; but because ye are not of the world, but I have chosen you out of the world, therefore the world hateth you. (John 15:18-19)

The world never has, nor ever will have, according to Christ, an interest in the things of God. The more highly esteemed a man is in the sight of God, the more he is "despised and rejected of men," as was his Savior. The illusion of a Great Last Days Revival makes for an interesting fantasy novel, but it has no place in the Scriptures. Toward the end of the age, the world will grow progressively worse, not better, and anyone who openly names the name of Christ will be targeted for persecution (2 Timothy 3:12). The Bible does indeed state that His followers will be brought before kings, but they will be in chains, and from imprisonment and the scaffold will face the same derision heaped upon the Savior while He was on the cross.

This desire for the church to have such worldly influence is nothing new. This has been the ambition of the Roman Catholic Church for centuries. That such prophecies would be unquestioningly accepted by Christians is amazing. This is a sign to us to show just how far we have been conditioned by MSOG concepts. But then again, thinking you're going to be welcomed before the world's rulers is much more comforting than "Nevertheless, when the Son of man cometh, shall he find faith on the earth?" (Luke 18:8).

I can't emphasize enough the man-centered nature of both the Latter Rain/MSOG doctrine and the prophetic movement that came out of it. Supposedly, by accepting these new prophets and their "words," we, the church, can usher in the presence of the

Lord, supposedly, for it is only after our triumph over the enemies of Christ that He will be "released" to return. Hamon states:

> When the church has put under it's feet all the enemies of Christ that he has ordained for them to subdue, then Christ can be released from heaven to return as the Manifested Head of His Physically Resurrected and Translated Church.[4]

The Toronto Blessing and the Pensacola Revival that came out of it have both been heavily influenced by prophetic ministries. Both of them claim to have been the result of prophecies given by David Yonggi Cho, the pastor of the world's largest Christian congregation in South Korea. They are also both seen by many as being the direct fulfillment of many of Paul Cain's and Bob Jones' prophecies, as is Promise Keepers. The new prophets are frequently given platforms in these and similar meetings.

Marc Dupont

THE TORONTO AIRPORT VINEYARD actually had its own "in house" prophet, long before the Toronto Blessing hit. His name is Marc Dupont, and he had prophesied in 1992 that "Like Jerusalem, Toronto will be center from which many are sent out to the nations," and that leaders would come from around the world to receive from the anointing there. He prophesied again in 1993 that he "sensed from the Lord an extreme danger for leaders who continue to resist the Holy Spirit," concerning the coming revival in Toronto. Interestingly, all of this occurred before there was any "Toronto Blessing."

Today, Dupont is president of Mantle of Praise Ministries, which states on its website:

> MoPM is a trans-denominational ministry concerned with building up the whole body of Christ, to help equip

and encourage the Church to do the work of Christ, and prepare for His return.[5]

Toronto's John Arnott currently sits on the Board of Mantle of Praise.

Marc Dupont's prophetic message calls for revival on the grounds that the church has become dull, uninspiring, and, worse yet, "religious." Another critique that he has frequently offered is that the church is more interested in the Bible than they are in the person of Jesus. He says that, "The churches are basically houses of Bible study, and not of prayer." ("Holy Ghost Train," cassette message).

To Dupont, church leaders are all too often guilty of resistance to the Holy Ghost, but the Holy Ghost will not be deterred, for Dupont asserts:

> The Holy Spirit has been rude enough to start ministry on His own without consulting the speakers.[6]

Dupont also criticizes intellectualism in the church as a hindrance to revival. In a taped message titled, "The Father's Heart and the Prophetic" Dupont places the blame for the fall of man on intellectualism and teaches that the barrenness of Michal, David's wife, Saul's daughter, was also a result of the same. He states:

> There is a barrenness because we have been clinging to ourselves, we've been trying to control the situation. It's as if with our continual focus on teaching, teaching, preaching . . . filling ourselves up.

When Dupont and others equate teaching and preaching with barrenness (in their own teachings), they set up an artificial tension between knowing Jesus and the knowledge of God (theology). It's as if those who seek the knowledge of God are dry and dead, while those who reject theology for unmediated experience are assumed to be "heart people" who truly know God. Dupont suggests this very thing when he states:

> We [Christians] love the truth about Jesus more than we love Jesus Himself.

The cumulative effect of this steady stream of teaching is cynicism and discontented unbelief, which breaks down any reasonable objections to the ministry of these "New Breed" prophets. The last shreds of discernment are further torn down by constant charges like the following:

> Christians have more confidence in Satan or the Antichrist to deceive us than we have in the Holy Spirit to lead us and guide us into all truth.[7]

What can one do? When large numbers of Christians have already assented to the charge that the church is dead, religious, uptight, critical, and even Pharisaical, and all this from a man widely received as a prophet from God, then the spiritual void created by this mindset must be filled with something. Nature abhors a vacuum. If it's perceived that the "old" way of church can no longer provide correct structure, interpretation, or teaching of the Scriptures, then a new order of things is the way to go. Let's face it—if you don't trust anyone who's involved with the "legalistic" church to properly handle the Word of God, then you'll find someone who you deem worthy. The safety perimeter of the Scriptures has effectively been removed There is no objective standard, at that point, from which to judge what is of God and what is not. Or even whether a particular prophet speaks from the Lord or from his own heart. It's a hallmark of the new prophets that either a Christian is for them and their teachings or he (the Christian) is opposing God. No middle ground is allowed. For all their talk about "unity" in the body of Christ, the new prophets create a divisiveness that can tear even good congregations apart. And through manipulative tactics, they put enough fear in followers that they will not speak up or challenge the prophets.

Both Dupont and Rick Joyner have been very effective in shaming God's people away from critical thinking. When Dupont says things like the following statement, he sets up a false tension between the Word of God and the character of God:

> [W]e can understand how it works in our heads . . . but God is not God the Father, God the Son and God the Holy Bible.[8]

The fact is, God's character is revealed by the Bible. It is the only objective method for determining what is of God, and if what we are feeling at a particular moment of prayer or worship is indeed the God who saved us through Jesus Christ. The Scriptures are absolutely essential to our relationship with Christ. Anything else is merely a feel-good religion, based on emotional and even esoteric experiences.

For those who still hold out against the rising tide of mysticism, an increasingly ominous tone to the many prophecies prevails as in this quote by Dupont:

> And so at the same time that churches that are responding to the Spirit are going to get more and more filled up with freedom and liberty and joy, and the peace and everything in the Kingdom. I believe that there's also going to come stricter and stricter judgement. I believe judgement (this year is radically increasing, especially leaders that are going to stand in a Pharisaical stance and are going to attack what God is doing.[9]

And what constitutes a "Pharisaical stance?" If anything, it seems not to be a description of those who oppose Jesus Christ and salvation by grace, as the real Pharisees. Rather, according to the prophets, it is those who offer valid criticism of the mysticism that has exploded on the earth with the advent of the Toronto Blessing. These new prophets pronounce judgment as if their concept of what God is doing in the latest "revival" is on the same level as the coming of Jesus to save us from our sins. It is biblical to pronounce judgment on those who reject Jesus or on those who pervert the Gospel of salvation by grace, for the Bible itself tells us in Hebrews 2:3, "How shall we escape, if we neglect so great salvation?" But it is reprehensible to pronounce that same judgment on God-fearing pastors and rank-and-file Christians, who actually preach the Gospel and love Jesus but whose only "fault" is their failure to recognize movements like the Toronto Blessing, and the Pensacola Outpouring as valid moves of God, or to recognize people like Rodney Howard Browne as a bona fide prophet. Dupont says:

> By the late nineties . . . Judgement is very much going to increase to the point where I believe that many leaders who are fighting what the Spirit of God is doing and saying, God is going to take them out of the ministry. I believe some of them, I know this isn't new, other people have said this, but I do believe it's true, that God is going to be taking some leaders home to heaven, rather than continue to allow them to mislead God's people.[10]

If critical thinking, à la the Bereans, is a vice to these people, openness to a wide array of extreme manifestations is a virtue. To use the word "extreme" is not engaging in hyperbole. The expression "Laughing Revival" doesn't do justice to the actual experiences of many. Perhaps a more apt term would be the Mystical Revival. Again, Dupont makes his position clear:

> God is not a gentleman, God is God! God is not the great I WAS or I WILL BE, right now, the dirty now and now, not the sweet by and by. Quite often when God's Spirit comes it is a little more than crazy. How the Son of God comes on people! I've seen glasses fly across the

room, I've seen marriage bands fly off fingers, I've seen boots and shoes fly off people, we've seen people destroy their clothes, almost being thrashed by the Holy Spirit.

Really? Does this sound like the Holy Spirit? The very Spirit of Truth who came to lead us into all truth? This is more reminiscent of the account in Acts 19 of the seven sons of Sceva. This is not to say that the Holy Spirit is a passive Being who never causes disruption and upheaval. He is part of the Godhead—sovereign, all-powerful, and He cannot be controlled. However, we do have a frame of reference with which to critically evaluate what are called "manifestations of the Spirit."

The impartation concept, introduced in the Latter Rain Revival, is alive and well, and with quite a bit of intensity in Dupont's experience, as he states:

It's one of the more scary things I've ever seen as 300 people were receiving 'major prophetic impartations' and were being shaken like rag dolls.

I want to emphasize at this point that it is neither my intention nor my responsibility to judge the motives of prophets such as Dupont and Joyner, who both may be sincerely attempting to be obedient to the Lord. Sincerity is no safeguard against deception, however. There is definitely something spiritual and powerful working in these ministries. People who have been touched by them have been radicalized. Can you imagine how hard you would have to be shaken to thrash off your wedding ring? To destroy your clothes? But what spirit is working here? Three hundred people being shaken like rag dolls? Why didn't Peter and Paul minister this?

The Campbells

WES AND STACEY CAMPELL, from British Columbia, were very much involved in the Toronto Blessing in its earlier days. Today, the

Campbells are faculty members at the [Peter] Wagner Leadership Institute and founders of RevivalNOW!

Wes Campbell testified of the sudden inundation of his church with the prophetic, well before the Toronto Blessing. I quote him in my book *Weighed and Found Wanting, Putting the Toronto Blessing in Context,* where he relates the supposed channeling of the Holy Spirit through a man in the church. When the man would come into the influence of the "Spirit," they would be able to ask "God" questions, which would be answered through the man's utterances. That this would be an accepted form of divine communion is an example of the level of discernment on which many have operated. God doesn't channel; He is not "trying to say something." God " . . . hath in these last days spoken unto us by his Son" (Hebrews 1:2). Jesus is the complete revelation of God, for He said, "he that hath seen me hath seen the Father" (John 14:9). When we look at Jesus in the Scriptures, the character of God becomes clear. The church doesn't need a human oracle to answer questions posed by a sign-seeking generation.

Stacy Campbell, Wes' wife, is considered to be a prophetess in the movement spurred by the Toronto Blessing, and there are several widely distributed prophecies which feature her prophesying while she whips her head about violently uttering breathlessly. It sends an otherworldly chill down the spine to see it, bringing to mind the Delphic Oracle. She also, as Bob Jones, Rick Joyner, and James Ryle, has prophesied of a coming "Civil War" in the church.

In Stacey Campbell's book *Praying the Bible: The Pathway to Spirituality: Seven Steps to a Deeper Connection with God,* Campbell leads her readers through the steps of contemplative mystical prayer in a chapter titled "Silent Contemplation," offering suggestions such as "practicing the Presence of God" by repeating what is known as the Jesus Prayer over and over to the point that one "can no longer live without it." She gives one example of a anonymous nineteenth-century Russian peasant who said the prayer 12,000 times a day in order to "pray without ceasing"! Campbell refers to an ancient collection of texts called *The Philokalia* written by "spiritual masters" between the 4th and 15th centuries about monastic spirituality (i.e., mysticism). Campbell's book explains that The Philokalia "contains clear explanations of what the Bible holds in secret and which cannot be easily grasped by our shortsighted understanding." This extra-biblical teaching of contemplative meditation leads practitioners into altered states of consciousness as practiced by the ancient Desert Fathers and brought forth in modern days by Catholic monks such as Thomas Merton, Basil Pennington, and Thomas Keating. These three monks held to a view that God exists in all people and this realization can be obtained in a person's life by this mantra-like meditation.

Stacey Campbell isn't the only modern-day "prophet" who has incorporated this mystical spirituality into her teachings. The Kansas City Prophets, for one, have promoted this for many years. Because of the esoteric experiences that happen in contemplative prayer and the highly subjective experiences within the Word Faith/Manifest Sons of God/Latter Rain movements, it was inevitable that the two would find a connection. And both the contemplative and the hyper-charismatic movements put "hearing the voice of God" above truth found in the Scriptures. But are they really hearing the voice of God? I don't believe they are but are rather entertaining familiar spirits.

James Ryle

THE PASTOR OF THE Boulder Vineyard, and mentor to Bill McCartney of Promise Keepers, is also a prophet. His name is James Ryle. He is an important guru in our discussion of the modern day prophets because of his wide influence, which can be seen through Promise Keepers, as well as through his books on the subject of prophecy and dream interpretation, *Hippo in the Garden* and *A Dream Come True*. Perhaps one of his best known and most controversial prophecies was given in a message entitled "Sons of Thunder." Ryle prophesied that the Beatles (as in John, Paul,

George, and Ringo) were at one time anointed by the Holy Spirit to bring in worldwide revival through music.

> [Quotes Psalm 68:18] . . . The Lord spoke to me and said, "What you saw in the Beatles—the gifting and the sound they had-was from Me. It did not belong to them, it belonged to Me. And it was My purpose to bring forth through music a worldwide revival that would usher in the move of my Spirit in bringing in men and women to Christ . . . And I want to tell you those four lads, they aborted something. They took what did not belong to them and used it in a way that was not intended by God to be used. It did bring in a revival of music, but it brought it on the other side of the fence—if you know what I am saying." And the Lord spoke to me and He said, "In 1970 I lifted the anointing off of them. And it has been held in my hand ever since . . . that anointing belongs to the church."[11]

Ryle's message goes on to say that he saw a vision of a Sergeant Pepper's Lonely Hearts Club Band record jacket floating down and he knew that represented the anointing, the mantle, the covering that was coming to the "Sons of Thunder." "And not long ago, the Lord said, 'I'm giving you permission to pass the jacket out.'"

Need we say any more of this widely acclaimed prophet? John Wimber prophesied that Ryle would be a seer to the Body of Christ, and in that same year, Ryle had a dream of a hippo standing in a garden, which was interpreted to mean that a new prophetic movement would be sweeping the church and impacting the whole world. (Charisma, Aug.1993, "James Ryle: From Prisoner to Preacher").

THERE ARE MANY OTHERS who are prominent in this prophetic movement; these, here, are a mere sampling. Hundreds and even thousands have been touched and influenced by William Branham,

The Kansas City Prophets, Rick Joyner, Paul Cain, James Ryle, Morris Cerullo, Earl Paulk, Bill Hamon, and dozens of others who are vigorously promoting the movement of new prophets and apostles.

How should the church respond to them? Are there reliable, objective tests to which the church can submit them? What do these prophets say about these biblical tests? What is a responsible theology of the prophetic?

These are some of the questions for which we, the church of our Lord Jesus Christ, desperately need answers.

10

Judging Prophetic Ministry

Despise not prophesyings. Prove all things; hold fast that
which is good. (1 Thessalonians 5:20-21)

I think that the church . . . is reacting in fear today . . .
people are saying, "Oh be careful, be careful! . . . be
careful what you read, be careful who lays hands on you"
. . . but if you play it safe with this thing, the Holy Spirit,
you know what? You're never going to get anywhere . . .
See we need to have more faith in God's ability to bless
then Satan's ability to deceive.[1]

THE TWO QUOTES ABOVE illustrate for us the contrasting views of
an approach to New Testament prophecy and prophetic ministry.
In the New Testament, as I read it, we are commanded not to
despise prophesying. On the other hand, the New Testament does
not support current charismatic attitudes, for we are emphatically
commanded to "Try [test] all things." And the Bible is very clear
that not everything that says it is of God is.

Today, there is an abuse and manipulation of people in the
name of the work of the Holy Spirit. Those who manipulate God's
people into passive acceptance of unscriptural practices have become adept at labeling the discerning believers as "religious" or
"in reaction," or even comparing them to unbelievers. The truth
is, to believe Jesus is to take seriously His admonition that "there

shall arise false Christs . . . "insomuch that, if it were possible, they shall deceive the very elect." (Matthew 24:24). Note, He said false "Christs" not false "Jesus.'" Why is this signicant? The current proclamation is that many are now operating under a new anointing, never before experienced in the church but now revealed for the "Last-Days, cutting-edge church." This is not a new Jesus, but a new anointing. The word *Christ* is a transliteration of the Greek word that means "Anointed One." A "false Christ" is nothing more or less than a falsely anointed one.

It is at least suspect for so-called spokesmen for God to be shaming people out of critically evaluating the new spiritual experiences that continually spring forth. This is especially so when such strong claims have been made of them by their proponents. Anything so signicant that to resist it is to endanger one's life, ministry and in some cases his very salvation should at least call for some biblical scrutiny. These are the very claims being made by the leaders in "the River," the Toronto Blessing, the Prophetic movement, and so forth. The severest and most fervent railings have been hurled at those who would dare raise questions.

Sadly, multitudes of Christians have fallen for these threats, thus remaining silent while following the pided piper into spiritual deception. What a contrast to the Bible, which declares of the Bereans that they were "noble" because they wouldn't blindly accept the apostle Paul's teachings until they had thoroughly investigated them through intensive Bible study. They rightly acknowledged that, as Christians, we are actually commanded to judge all things and cling tightly to anything that is good and abhor that which is evil. Paul stated this in the context of New Testament prophecy!

In order to offer a biblical perspective, it is helpful to outline a few things. First, there is a difference between the gift of prophecy and the prophetic offce. Acts 21 brings the contrast out for us, for in speaking of the evangelist Philip, it states:

> And the same man had four daughters, virgins, which did prophesy. (Acts 21:9)

But in the next verse we learn that,

> And as we tarried there many days, there came down from
> Judea a certain prophet, named Agabus. (Acts 21:10)

There is a difference between those who stand in a Pentecostal worship service and believe they have received an utterance to, "edification, and exhortation, and comfort" (1 Corinthians 14:3), and someone who assumes the position of an Agabus, an Elijah, Isaiah or a Jeremiah. In the gift of prophecy, an utterance may or may not have been given to them to encourage the Body, or it may have been them thinking they had a "word from the Lord" when it really wasn't God at all. This can be corrected, and 1 Corinthians brings this out. God gives people utterances, encouragements, thoughts, impressions etc.

However, being used to prophesy to edification, exhortation and comfort is a far cry from assuming the role of a prophet of the Living God! If I fail to receive a prophecy in a church service, I have cheated myself out of perhaps some much-needed encouragement. But, if I disregard a prophet that the Lord sent unto me, that is a serious matter! Therefore, it is a far more serious thing to proclaim yourself to be a prophet, than it is to be used to give an encouraging utterance in a church. When Kenneth Hagin gave his message, "How To Write Your Own Ticket With God," he didn't say that he found this teaching in Scripture. If he had, we would be in a position to possibly debate it or accept it or even think, "He's a good man, but I don't agree with his interpretation of Scripture." We don't have that option, for Hagin tells us, Jesus himself appeared to him and taught him this! At this point it's not a matter of biblical interpretation. Hagin, who bills himself as a prophet of God, is presenting this as direct revelation from Jesus Christ Himself. This forces earnest and God-fearing believers to have to decide, "If I believe that Jesus told him this, I am bound to have to live by it, but if Jesus didn't tell him this, he is either lying, in the name of the Lord, or he really did have a spiritual experience, but was wrong about its source." Now if the latter is true, then what spirit appeared to Hagin teaching him (and us) things that supposedly are about God? And what spirit is claiming to be Jesus?

Can you see the dilemma here? We don't have the luxury to grant that we don't accept the particular interpretation, but Hagin is still a man of God. When people come forth with open dreams, visions, revelations, interactions with angels, and unmediated experiences in places like the throne room of God, whether we accept the responsibility or not, we are all forced into making a serious determination. Either they are "right on" or else they are "way off," of God or of the devil. There can be no middle ground.

This goes for predictions also. When New Testament prophets made predictions, they always came to pass. For example, Agabus predicted a "great dearth throughout all the world: which came to pass in the days of Claudius Caesar" (Acts 11:28). He was also used of God to warn Paul of the plots of the Jews to bind him in Acts 21-10-11. This also came to pass. Predictions in the name of the Lord are very serious business, as Deuteronomy 18 points out, and if there was some kind of new leniency toward inaccurate predictions in the New Testament, why are there no inaccurate predictions recorded there?

Do I believe there are prophets living today? Absolutely! The ascension gift ministries of Ephesians 4:11 are needed now more than ever. But we must take another look at the function of prophets in the Bible, and get away from the modern model of a prophet. The prophets of the Bible—Isaiah, Jeremiah, Daniel, John the Baptist, Agabus, and the prophets mentioned in Acts 13—were not those who went around having conferences, giving everyone personal "words," praying for inner healings, zapping people, cursing their detractors, etc. Prophets were and are preachers and teachers raised up for the purpose of calling God's people back to Him when they have fallen away. In the process of those teachings and preachings, predictions were made that attested to the validity of the messengers, and their message. Certainly there are prophets these days, and God validates their ministries as He sees fit. But the signs and wonders are not ends in themselves. The most important part is the message.

Another important distinction is the fact that Ephesians 2:20 has been fulfilled once and for all. It states,

> And [ye] are built upon the foundation of the apostles and prophets, Jesus Christ Himself being the chief corner stone.

Why is this an important distinction? Because this verse is currently being interpreted by many to mean that your very spiritual foundation rests upon the teachings of these new prophets, and to fail to submit to their ministries is to somehow leave you without a foundation. The apostles and prophets that the whole church is founded upon are the prophets of the Old Testament and the Apostles of the New. These are your foundation. Everything should be "plumbed" according to the apostles who wrote the New Testament and anything which contradicts their teaching is not of God. As it is written:

> We are of God: he that knoweth God heareth us: he that is not of God heareth not us. Hereby know we thespirit of truth, and the spirit of error. (1 John 4:6)

The God of the Bible is not currently "trying to say something to the church." He has already spoken to us through His Son (Hebrews 1:2). He has given us a "more sure word of prophecy; whereunto ye do well that ye take heed" (2 Peter 1:19). That Word is final and authoritative. Any genuine modern prophet is going to be raised up to call people back to that sure Word, even as Isaiah and Jeremiah were used to summon the children of Israel back to Moses, and to faithfulness to the God of Israel. Their messages were straight out of the Pentateuch (I exchanged "Torah" for "Pentateuch" here because, in the broadest sense, Torah can mean the written tradition of the Jews, including teachings of their rabbis. "Pentateuch" means, specifically, the first five books of the Bible). They preached sermons, expounded on the broken Law of God, the applications of His Holy penalties, the beauty of His attributes, and the main theme, Christ Himself! In the process of all of this they did indeed make predictions, which always related to the Messiah, and to God's purposes for Israel and the nations.

This linkage of prophets with teachers and preachers carries right over into the New Testament. When Peter warned that "There were false prophets also among the people, even as there shall be false teachers among you" (2 Peter 2:1), he wasn't confining this to the early church. This is extremely important to us, for the tests that Moses gave us for true or false prophets in Deuteronomy also carry over and are assumed in the New Testament. When the apostles said "prove (test) all things" or "try the spirits" (1 John 4:1), they were assuming that there was a basic familiarity with the tests, for there is no elaborate description of them. Thankfully, though the tests carry over, the penalty does not, for the church is not a theocratic entity as was the nation of Israel. We don't stone false prophets though the sin is no less serious! Certainly, false prophecy brings spiritual death and disillusionment wherever it is allowed unchecked.

There are two tests for prophets in Deuteronomy, one in chapter 13 and the other in chapter 18. Chapter 18 is the more simple and straightforward of the two:

> When a prophet speaketh in the name of the LORD, if the thing follow not, nor come to pass, that is the thing that the LORD hath not spoken, but the prophet hath spoken it presumptuously: thou shall not be afraid of him. (Deuteronomy 18:22).

As I said, this is very simple. God's prophets are 100% accurate in their pronouncements. God wants his flock to be able to tell right away who is and isn't of God. He is not giving you an ambiguous, subjective test here, such as "Does he seem to love Jesus?," which can be easily faked. For a literal example of this, in 1994, Paul and Jan Crouch hosted a prophet named John Hinkle on their show who predicted that on June 9th of that year, "All evil would be ripped off of the earth." Obviously, by June 10, it should have been obvious to all that Hinkle's pronouncement was a false prophecy. It should have been, of course, but these days the conditioning has been so consistent that many were hard pressed to know what to do about it! This man seemed so loving and sincere that apparently it was difficult to openly correct him. It's as if we expect false prophets to have fangs and wear a long black cape.

So many have already been disillusioned, and some have even lost their faith because of this toleration of false prophets! The prophets themselves, in many cases, after having dabbled at being a "seer," intoxicated by the power that many attribute to them, have gone on to shipwreck their own faith. Adding insult to injury the New Breed of prophets have devised ingenious ways of theologizing around the tests that the Lord instituted for His flock's safety, and also they have turned the responsibility for their failed prophecies back on to the recipients of them. How many times has a disappointed believer been subtly reprimanded with the excuse that the prophecy didn't come to pass "because you lacked faith"? Talk about kicking a man when he's down. The "prophecy" never had a chance at fulfillment in the first place, because it was not of God, and when the obvious happens, it's the recipient's fault!

The second test for true and false prophets is more subtle. Suppose you have a prophet whose predictions do come to pass? His words to people seem accurate, he seems to have the power to heal, and people seem to be supernaturally helped after he "ministers." Can we now automatically assume that all is well? Is God indeed blessing and endorsing this ministry? Not necessarily. Hear what the Scriptures say:

If there arise among you a prophet, or a dreamer of dreams, and giveth thee a sign or a wonder, and the sign or the wonder come to pass, whereof he spake unto thee saying, "Let us go after other gods, which thou hast not known, and let us serve them"; thou shalt not hearken unto the words of that prophet, or that dreamer of dreams: for the LORD your God proveth you, to know whether ye love the LORD your God with all your heart and with all your soul. (Deuteronomy 13:1-3)

Of course it should be obvious that very few false prophets would come into a Christian church and announce, "Let us go after other gods and serve them!" In fact, I am convinced that most false prophets have no idea, either that they are leading people after false gods, or that they are indeed false prophets! Deuteronomy 13 calls our attention to a principle, that when seeking to determine the validity of a ministry, which in this case is that of prophets, we are not to focus on the "signs and wonders" nor the "results," to the exclusion of focusing on the message, and the accompanying teaching. Remember that signs, wonders, predictions, and other results of any ministry only attest to the message that particular ministry brings. They are not ends in themselves. These days the focus is very much upon the spectacular, the miracles or the promise of them. Deuteronomy ought to alert us to the fact that in some instances, God will actually allow false prophets to arise and seem to "have the goods," that He might test His people, to see if they "Love the LORD their God with all of their heart."

Love God? Of course we love God! We have never had such zeal and love, and the church has never been so "on fire." There has never been such an abundance of worship in all of church history! But this is loving God on our terms, and not God's. How do you know you truly love God? To God, love is translated as loyalty, and loyalty to His Word.

Alas, as in the days of William Branham, we are currently minimizing the teachings of the new prophets and maximizing their alleged signs and wonders. We are so generous though, for when some prophet does make an inaccurate prediction, or brings forth some outrageously unorthodox teaching, we grant that "He may get a little off at times, but his heart is in the right place, and God seems to be endorsing him, as he so obviously has 'the power'." We have been given numerous opportunities to pass the Deuteronomy 13 test, as Pentecostals and Charismatics, but we seem to continuously flunk them.

We have mentioned William Branham as an example of a clear-cut Deuteronomy 13 test. There were many Pentecostal leaders who sought to convince Branham to play down his unorthodox teachings, so that he could continue to gain acceptance in Pentecostal churches. As long as he stayed with his sign gift ministry, and didn't teach too much, they figured it didn't matter what he personally believed, as "people are getting results." For some time Branham actually did limit his extreme revelations to his own Jeffersonville, Indiana congregation. He downplayed his "Serpent's Seed" revelation and his abhorrence of the doctrine of the Trinity, so that he would be accepted in "Trinitarian" churches. Today, unfortunately, the lesson of William Branham is still largely misunderstood. The popular opinion is that Branham didn't have a teaching ministry, so he should have avoided teaching; that he missed his calling as a prophet and a healer, not a teacher. To such devotees the lesson is, "Don't stray out of your calling."

Wrong!!! We, the church, should be shouting from the housetops, "Prophets are teachers and preachers, and they always have a message. Don't judge them by their 'results,' but by their message! Just because they can make accurate predictions or tell you something about your life, or even heal you, doesn't mean they are sent by God!"

It is so easy to forget that Mormons have signs and wonders as well. Failing marriages have come together, people have quit smoking, and there have been former degenerates who became upright citizens as a result of Mormonism! But it is of the spirit of Antichrist! The fruit of a prophet, a movement, or a revival can be evaluated by the consistent teaching. (Matthew 12:33-35).

Well, of course Branham had never gotten up and said, "Let us go after other gods." As far as I can tell he was a profoundly sincere and humble man. But again, so was Edgar Cayce. However, the god of Branham's Angel, is not the God of the Bible. The god who inspired the Serpent's Seed teaching, with its hatred of women and its racial undertones is certainly not the God of the Bible. The spirit who told Branham that the Zodiac, the Great Pyramid, and the Scriptures were all valid words from God, is definitely not the Holy Spirit. Nor is the god of Rodney Howard Browne's "Holy Ghost Bartender" ministry, or the god of Rick Joyner's talking Eagle, Bob Jones' Civil War, and his "Dominus" vision. The spirit who taught James Ryle that the Beatles were anointed by the Holy Spirit until 1970 (the year they broke up), is not the God of Daniel and Isaiah. The Jesus who told Kenneth Hagin how he could "write his own ticket with God" is certainly not Jesus the Messiah. The God of the Bible is not localizing Himself in cities like Pensacola or Toronto, so that little churches all over the world can charter buses there to get "it" (the anointing). But if we were to go by external "results," all of these are validated by signs and wonders, changed lives, healings and bad habits being broken. It is not our place to judge their motives either positively or negatively, but it is our responsibility to judge the message.

John, in 1 John 4:3, confirms this test, when he puts forth a doctrinal standard for prophets.

> . . . and every spirit that confesseth not that Jesus Christ is come [and remains] in the flesh is not of God: and this is that spirit of antichrist.

This is the New Testament version of Deuteronomy 13, warning us that the Antichrist can be known by a consistent teaching which spiritualizes the person of Jesus. The word "confesseth" does not refer to an ability or inability to say "Jesus has come and remains in the flesh," but rather it refers to the consistent teaching of the ministry. For example, a Jehovah's Witness, when pressed, can easily say the confession of the incarnation, but when the overall doctrine is evaluated, there is exposed a consistent denial of the incarnation, that God came to us in the flesh, in the person of Jesus Christ.

In summary, the tests for the validity of a prophet are found in chapters 13 and 18 of the Book of Deuteronomy. Prophets are to be regarded not as wonder workers, giving personal words, blowing people away with signs and wonders, but always as messengers. Therefore, it is not the results, but the prophet's message that justifies or condemns the prophetic ministry. That message is always either humanistic, demonic, or a Word from the God of Scripture. God will test His people, from time to time, on their love. Love on His terms means loyalty to His truth.

11

Prophetic Evasion

The prophet who misses it occasionally in his prophecies may be ignorant, immature, or presumptuous, or he may be ministering with too much zeal and too little wisdom and anointing. But this does not prove him a false prophet. . . . it is certainly possible for a true prophet to be inaccurate.[1]

When it comes to something such as personal prophecy, we believe that extremism is more deadly than when dealing with less volatile issues. That is because there is an element of control involved when one individual is able to speak for God to a group of individuals . . . We believe there are some who purport to prophesy that actually get their unusual ability to know the future, not from the Holy Spirit, but from the Spirit of Divination. And there are some Charismatics who are so eager to know God's will or get a Word from God or to be singled out in a service where this special gift may be manifest that they are susceptible to spirits that are not from God.[2]

How interesting that the editor of *Charisma* magazine (a magazine which promotes the Apostles and Prophets movement) acknowleges the danger of this movement. But he sure got it right here!

One consistent characteristic of the new prophets is their insistence that they do not have to be subjected to the

Deuteronomy tests. They are incredibly resourceful in the many ways they rationalize this position. But, for those who accept their reasoning, the end result is that there is no objective standard with which to measure them. I have assembled a sampling of the new prophets' quotes on this subject so that rather than tell you what they are saying, you can see for yourself in their own words how they approach the subject of prophetic accountability. As Rick Joyner notes:

> One of the greatest hazards affecting maturing prophets is the erroneous interpretation of the Old Testament exhortation that if a prophet ever predicted something which did not come to pass he was no longer to be considered a true prophet . . . The warning was that if this happened, the prophet has been presumptuous and the people were not to fear him. If one predicts something in the name of the Lord and it does not come to pass, he probably has spoken presumptuously and needs to be repented of, but that does not make him a false prophet. No one could step out in the faith required to walk in his calling if he knew that a single mistake could ruin him for life.[3].

How is it erroneous to interpret Moses as saying that we are to reject inaccurate prophets? If the church is to provoke Israel to jealousy (Romans 10:19), by in the inheritance which has been temporarily suspended from Israel, how could inaccurate prophets possibly provoke the people of Moses to jealousy? And what about the person to whom the false prophecy is directed? Joyner conveniently neglects to point out that many a poor soul received a false prophecy that "could ruin him for life."

Joyner's line of reasoning is utter nonsense. In the above quote, he seems to be suggesting that invalidating a supposed prophet's "calling" makes the prophet a victim, instead of the recipient. Let's be very clear here. False prophecies can easily destroy lives. When a man receives what he believes is a genuine "word of the Lord," then he will align his life accordingly. If the personal prophecy is false, then the instructions given to the recipient are also false, and the person then bases life decisions on carnal or even demonic instruction.

And we're supposed to feel sorry for prophets who "miss it?" The irony is staggering.

Joyner then appeals to Bob Jones's teaching on prophetic accuracy when he writes:

> Bob [Jones] was told that the general level of prophetic revelation in the church was about 65% accurate at this time. Some are only about 10% accurate, a very few of the most mature prophets are approaching 85% to 95% accuracy. Prophecy is increasing in purity, but there is a still a long way to go for those who walk in this ministry. This is actually grace for the church now, because 100% accuracy in this ministry would bring a level of accountability to the church which she is too immature to bear at this time. It would result in too many Ananiases and Sapphiras.[4]

Where do we begin to comment on this kind of reasoning? Let's start with the evolutionary view of prophets. It is "maturing" prophets who are being referenced, who as they mature, evolve or grow into an increasing level of accuracy. So, prophecy itself is evolving, "increasing in purity?" According to Jones and Joyner, yes. It is a good thing, too! For if we were presently at the 100% level, there would be corpses all over churches around the world! Think Ananias and Sapphira! Accepting this kind of thinking would actually make you grateful for inaccurate prophecy, as if it is a blessing. The example of Ananias and Sapphira is used over and over again to make people glad that we aren't quite at the 100% level yet. Remember, now—"100% accuracy in this ministry would bring a level of accountability to the church which she is too immature to bear at this time." Isn't that nice? These earnest men want to be accurate, and probably would be, but it is the church which holds it all back, for she is not quite "there yet." One must admit, these people are good at communication!

If the church isn't mature enough, at this time, for 100% prophecy, why didn't that stop God in the Book of Acts when Ananias and Sapphira actually did die? Was Israel more mature than we are now, in the days of Isaiah, Jeremiah and Ezekiel? Where are Peter's 30% prophecies or Agabus's 45% prophecies? What other prophets had been given the luxury to grow into 100% accuracy?

Another evasion is in the oft-used disclaimer that, "We aren't saying that we are prophets. We are only saying that we have a prophetic ministry." Mike Bickle, for example, in an interview in the book, *Some Said It Thundered*, which is a positive account of the Kansas City Prophets, is asked the question by the author David Pytches, "Do prophets ever get things wrong?"

> Mike Bickle was at pains to stress that he saw a real distinction between the recognized office of a prophet and those who received revelations and gave prophecies. At KCF they only actually regard Paul Cain as a prophet . . . though the self-effacing Paul would never claim such an offce for himself . . . We asked tactfully if any of them was ever wrong. They all agreed that they had occasionally been proved wrong. Sometimes their revelation was right but their interpretation or application was wrong.[5]

In my opinion, this amounts to a semantic evasion of the Deuteronomy tests, that somehow it's all right to stand up in the name of the Lord and speak to God's people, fully expecting to be received as authoritative, as long as you don't call yourself a prophet. Act like a prophet, tell the church you saw Jesus Christ in a vision and a dream, pass on to an enthralled audience the unique and intriguing "words" that this "Jesus" gave you . . . but when you are proven false, duck out of accountability by denying that you are technically a prophet! Such a form of rationalization leaves critical thinking lying, gasping in the dust.

It would be different if these people were merely sharing their "insights" of Scripture, for then there would be room for debate and discussion. They may, or may not have the correct insights. But these are not mere insights, but interactive visions, talking angels, authoritative words, predictions, etc. In many cases, we are cautioned that to reject these ministries is to endanger yourself to be another Ananias and Sapphira. These people speak out of both sides of their mouths. On the one hand, they allow themselves to be called prophets, they write books about the coming restoration of prophets, they posture themselves as prophets along the line of an Isaiah or a Daniel, and they make excuses for "maturing prophets," but when godly people want to apply valid scriptural tests to them, they deny being a prophet!

Branham, their mentor, did much the same thing. We see this in an excerpt from a book entitled *The Healer Prophet, William Marrion Branham*, by C. Douglas Weaver. The author states:

> Until the twilight of his ministry, Branham consistently denied that he was a prophet. When informed that he claimed the identity of a prophet while under the anointing, Branham responded, "You've heard me never as far as speaking I'd say, 'God made me his prophet.' I've heard people say on tape that they picked it up when the inspiration was on, but that was him speaking, not me, see. Better for Him to tell you then for me to tell you that. See?"[6]

In other words, Branham said, "I never said I was a prophet, but if I did it wasn't me. It was spoken under the anointing. It was Jesus that called me a prophet!" And who could argue with Jesus, right?

Al Dager in his *Media Spotlight Report* on the Kansas City Prophets, in 1990, states:

> Though these men have come to be recognized as prophets by some, Mike Bickle states that he does not recognize them as prophets in the truest sense of the word, but rather as men who have merely been gifted with a prophetic ministry: "There's no one in our midst that we give the title 'prophet.' The only one I would feel comfortable giving that office would be Paul Cain, but he refuses to accept it. So I'd say both of them—apostle and prophet—I believe that in God's purpose they exist, but we're very hesitant to designate somebody as being one at this point in time. But I believe that will be recognized in the future . . . I don't think that the men should go very heavy on calling themselves that; we definitely don't call the other prophetic guys prophets. I don't feel they have the stature of a prophet yet; I think they have a prophetic ministry, but I don't think they are actually at the level of a prophet."

Dager went on to say that despite his denials, Bickle had indeed been well-documented as calling these men "prophets," and that it is a fallacy to try to separate the prophetic ministry from the office of a prophet. Dager accurately observes:

> Every believer has a "prophetic ministry," because we all may receive a word from the Lord, usually a scripture to reprove, rebuke, exhort, or encourage one another. But this is not what these men practice; they claim a prophetic ministry similar to the Old Testament prophets: revealed knowledge gained from direct face to face encounters with God; they give directive prophecies to individuals, entire congregations, and to the church at large. They want the glory of a prophet, but not the responsibility.[7]

Not all deny the title "prophet" in their evasion of prophetic accountability; many just come right out and contradict Moses' instructions as not being applicable to a New Testament prophet.

> The prophet who misses it occasionally in his prophecies may be ignorant, immature, or presumptuous, or he may be ministering with too much zeal and too little wisdom and anointing. But this does not prove him a false prophet . . . it is certainly possible for a true prophet to be inaccurate. He would not do it knowingly, for a true prophet is so conscientious he would rather never speak at all than speak even one false word or give wrong direction to even one person. So we must understand the distinction between a false prophecy and a false prophet if we are to be open to what God says. One of the quickest ways to get into trouble with God is to accuse one of Christ's prophets falsely. When we do that, we are touching the very nerve of heaven, and we are sure to receive a very negative reaction. God says in His word, "Do my prophets no harm."[8]

Note that Hamon would remove the objective test of true and false prophets, and would have us test on an entirely subjective level, the prophet's motive. "A true prophet would not do it knowingly." Therefore, even if there are false and misleading prophecies, we are warned not to make a judgment, unless we can determine whether or not it was done knowingly. I doubt that Edgar Cayce "knowingly" was a false prophet. The same goes for Jean Dixon and Nostradamus. It is impossible for us to discern motive. Neither is it within our power or our responsibility. That is why we aren't given such a test in the Old and New Testaments.

The extent of this reconditioning of God's people to be more tolerant and accepting of false prophecy on the basis of motive is illustrated in an editorial in *Charisma* Magazine in December, 1994, entitled "When Prophecies Prove False," by Karen Howe.

The article was in response to the disillusionment many had felt, after believing the aforementioned June 9, 1994 prediction which John Hinkle had proclaimed on TBN, that on that date God would "Rip all evil off of the face of the earth." The author of the article held that the prediction seemed credible because it was verified by "two men with reliable ministries." Howe writes:

> Those of us who were stirred by the words of these men felt a strange mixture of grief (for the poor prophets), embarrassment (at being so gullible ourselves), disappointment (that we couldn't have the announced visitation from God), and frustration (because it's so hard to tell counterfeit gifts from authentic ones). It was especially discomforting for those of us foolish enough to share the prophecies with skeptical non-Christians . . . And I was once more, angry with God. This would not have happened, I decided, if He had either protected His prophets from false visions or had cooperated by fulfilling their words.

That this article should even have been taken seriously enough to be printed ought to be a wake up call that we in the Charismatic church have been so conditioned against critical thinking that we side more with false prophets than we do with the honor of God! That anybody would actually consider the use of such an obviously false prediction to evangelize skeptical friends is staggering! Another staggering thought is that the "poor prophets" are lauded and the anger was reserved for God, who failed to bail them out. Small wonder we are awash in false prophets. Not to worry, though, for the same article explains how the Holy Spirit gave the author a positive way to look at false prophecy, which included that it was wrong to be mad at God when a human vessel fails. Also, to see that in some cases, false prophecies are a temptation from Satan. But were the prophets false? Howe clears this up for us when she states:

I believe that the prophets who spoke this year were motivated by courage and caring, not by a desire to deceive. We should pray that their ministries will not suffer, and that the church's gifts of discernment and discretion will be strengthened against further mistakes.

This incredible article concludes by comparing the experience of the false prophecy of 1994 with the crucifixion of Jesus, who on the cross ". . . experienced the seeming contradiction of being abandoned by a God whose nature is to love, not to punish, to support his children, not turn away from them."

THERE WILL BE A tremendous price paid for our lack of loyalty to God and His Word; in fact it is already being paid by many who have submitted their lives to these new prophets. Jack Deere, in a teaching on prophetic ministry at the Toronto Airport Vineyard in November, 1994, acknowledged some of the pitfalls and reservations pastors have to opening their pulpits to "maturing prophets" when he said,

> Who in the world would be against that ministry? They don't want it in their churches because it causes messes . . . [begins to describe the experience of one young prophet in training] He's standing before a group of high school kids. And he starts out . . . and he's humbled, and he's a little frightened and kind of awed at the responsibility and he starts calling people out of the audience. And he starts getting it right and the people start oohing and aaahing, and his chest started coming out like this, and you see this garment of pride coming down, and then he calls out a young man of 18 or 19, and he says, "You're into pornography, and the Lord says you have to repent." The young man begins to cry. Sits back down. The only problem was the young man wasn't into pornography. He was publically humiliated before 800 high school kids. We had to go back to his church, apologize to

> his whole church . . . it was a horrible mess . . . But do
> you know what? God is in the process of offending our
> minds in order to reveal our hearts! And I don't know
> anyplace where He's going to give us a pure ministry. I
> don't know anyplace where it's going to be 100% right.
> There's going to be stumbling blocks in any ministry
> that the Holy Spirit is really responsible for.

It is amazing that after recounting that horror story of a blatant abuse of so-called prophecy, Deere's conclusion was the tired old mantra, popularized by John Wimber that "God is in the process of offending our minds to reveal our hearts." As in the *Charisma* article mentioned earlier, which defended the false prophet who gave the June 9th prophecy, another travesty is perpetrated on the Body of Christ, and the conclusion is that God is responsible for it. God is not libeling eighteen-year-old boys, accusing them of things they haven't done. Not the God of the Bible. No. There is another force at work here, about which Moses already warned us when, through him, the Lord referenced those who depart from the faith with their words of "Let us go after other gods which we have not known, and serve them . . ."

I assure you that with such a mindset, which can justify abuse of people in the name of "the prophetic," we will see a lot more of this, probably even going beyond false testimony against individuals. Whole churches will be attacked this way as long as these false prophets are allowed to continue "maturing" their gift on real people. The damage will prove to be incalculable in terms of individually shipwrecked believers, false converts, division in the Body, squandered opportunities to witness, and even wrecked churches. The refusal of our leadership, especially the Pentecostals, to rise up and rebuke this unfaithfulness, will be witness against them before the throne of God. Instead of laughing and mourning, we should be weeping! Alas, the scripture in Jeremiah 5:31 has come to pass in our day

The prophets prophesy falsely, and the priests bear rule by their means; and my people love to have it so.

God's people love it. They must love the idea of a "God's Bartender," a seer, who can serve them up personal and self-gratifying "words." It is nice to think that our generation is so special, that the apostles in heaven are lined up waiting to shake hands with our latter day apostles. These prophets have appealed to the vanity of a vain generation. The only Spirit they manifest is the Zeitgeist, the spirit of this vanishing age. This is particularly seen in their insistence that there should be no objective tests for them, no absolute by which to test their boastful claims, and that nothing or no one is wrong except those who dare challenge them by the Word of God! In many ways these are postmodern prophets; they don't speak for God, for as Jude 19 says, "these be they who separate themselves, sensual, having not the Spirit."

The justifications for false and inaccurate prophecies are endless, for there is a constant need for them. One of the most creative I've seen was given by Bob Jones in an interview with Mike Bickle, on the widely distributed tape, "The Shepherd's Rod."

> [Jones]: The Rhema will be two thirds right on. Not quite time for Ananias and Sapphira yet.

> [Bickle]: The Lord actually said that sentence to you?

> [Jones]: Yeah, I mean what he was really showing me was, "I'm going to release the Rhema to where that many begin to move two-thirds right on with their words, and the other third will be like poppin' a bullet at the enemy and he wouldn't fire. It was a blank." And He [God] said, "I'm the one that's loading the gun, so there's going to be some blanks there . . . the blanks is pointed in the general direction of the enemy anyway"

> . . . "If I [God] release the 100% Rhema right now,
> the accountability would be so awesome and you'd have
> so much Ananias and Sapphira's going on the people
> couldn't grow."

This is an amazing statement, which makes God responsible for the "blanks" (false prophecies) and gives Him a reason for deceiving us! Jones would actually make you feel relieved and thankful for false prophecy, using the old Ananias and Sapphira threat. We must be a special generation, we are the first one ever, that God supposedly protected from His 100% accurate Word! To this day, Bickle, the Vineyard and many others involved, consider Jones to be a "man with a very profound prophetic ministry."[9] At one point, Bickle himself admitted that Jones never should have been put on the front stage, that he should have been allowed to be some kind of "backstage" prophet. (See my book *Weighed and Found Wanting* for a fuller treatment of this false prophet).

What is going to become of us Pentecostals? Whether we know it or not, Satan has desired to have us that he may sift us as wheat (Luke 22:31). We are currently being tested for our love of God, our loyalty, and that love is as God defines it. If our Lord will have mercy on us, He will sober us up, for the times definitely don't call for spiritual drunkenness. We need to have clear heads for clear, biblical thinking. This has become a matter of loyalty to God and true spirituality. We don't have to choose between "Charismania" or deadness. It is just as sinful for the orthodox remnant of the church to have no passion for God, no life of worship, no love of people, as it is for the other side of the church to be so open to everything coming down the road.

As the psalmist cried out, "Who will rise up for me against the evildoers?" (Psalm 94:16). Will we shepherds ever be faithful and protect our flocks, regain our convictions and quit taking our signals from the most current religious fad? Will we be willing to be obscure, and toil thanklessly in the Lord's fields, or do we insist on being "with it?"

I am no prophet, but I will close for now with a prophecy.

> And I will gather the remnant of my flock out of all countries whither I have driven them, and will bring them again to their folds; and they shall be fruitful and increase. And I will set up shepherds over them which shall feed them; and they shall fear no more, nor be dismayed, neither shall they be lacking, saith the Lord . . . And I will give you pastors according to mine heart, which shall feed you with knowledge and understanding. (Jeremiah 23:3-4 and 3:15).

12

The Slide into the Occult...

For rebellion is as the sin of witchcraft, and stubbornness is as iniquity and idolatry. Because thou hast rejected the word of the Lord, he hath also rejected thee from being king.(1 Samuel 15:22)

And when Saul saw the host of the Philistines, he was afraid, and his heart greatly trembled. And when Saul enquired of the Lord, the Lord answered him not, neither by dreams, nor by Urim, nor by prophets. Then said Saul unto his servants, Seek me a woman that hath a familiar spirit, that I may go to her, and enquire of her. And his servants said to him, Behold, there is a woman that hath a familiar spirit at Endor. (1 Samuel 28:5-7)

THE TRAGIC STORY OF King Saul ought to serve as a warning to Bill Johnson, Rick Joyner and many of the other leaders of the Prophetic movement we have been discussing.

Though Saul had a promising beginning as the first king of Israel, he ended up in the occult, seeking a "word" from the witch of Endor. God was no longer speaking to him, neither directly nor through any prophets or priests, whom he had consistently disregarded, and had even killed in some cases. But "the show had to go on," as they say.

I see the Charismatic movement as being in the same position. I have no doubt that God was speaking to many of us in the renewal of the 1960s and 1970s and much of it was a genuine move of the Holy Spirit. Many were saved and experienced the gifts and ministry of the Holy Spirit through it.

But as the movement developed theologically, it soon came under the influence of false teachers and prophets. Rather than listening to those who have long tried to warn them of the danger of apostasy, Charismatic leaders turned their flocks over to various heretics and false prophets with "positive" messages of prosperity, Dominion and health.

This attitude, which disdained criticism and discernment, came about as a result of a misguided false toleration—a "love only" emphasis, very similar to the "new toleration" running rampant through the culture at the time. In spite of the scriptural command to "judge all things," Charismatic teaching at the time considered those judging any brother to be Pharisaic and hypocritical.

Thus the Charismatic movement grew into various manifestations; variously a Manifested Sons of God, Kingdom Now, Word Of Faith, Faith Prosperity movement, all of which eventually morphed into a "restoration of Apostles and Prophets" movement, a mystical Spiritual Warfare movement, a distorted "Laughing Revival" of spiritual drunkenness, and finally the experience-based Toronto/Pensacola "revivals" and their toxic offspring.

For those who have participated deeply in all of the above, it is hard to admit that they were wrong! As Nicodemus the teacher of Israel asked Jesus, "Can a man be born when he is old?" i.e., are you saying I have to admit I am wrong and start all over again?

Even after the fiasco involving the public "commendation of Todd Bentley" and the subsequent adultery and disgraceful abandonment of his wife and children, there has been virtually no soul searching by these NAR leaders.

None of the "Prophets" and "Apostles" seem to be questioning themselves—"Are we really hearing from God?," or "Should we really have endorsed this fraud?" Rather they are doubling down on their praise and endorsement of Todd.

How could ten of the "leading prophets" have been so publically repudiated by Bentley's deception?

Instead they have embraced an entire theology of the deconstruction of their critics, employing empty clichés such as: "They are afraid of the Supernatural." "They are jealous of us power people." "They criticize because they are into 'head knowledge' and are not in the Spirit." "They are Pharisees . . . religious hypocrites who don't have the goods, and are afraid of people who do." "Dead, dried up," and perhaps the worst accusation, "religious."

There has always been a Discernment movement (Walter Martin, Dave Hunt, Dave Wilkerson, John MacArthur, et al.) When Dave Hunt released his well-researched and documented book, *The Seduction of Christianity,* the Charismatic leaders openly disdained him, calling upon their followers not to read his book as it would "disturb their spirits."

Bill Johnson and the rest of the "Apostles and Prophets" of the NAR would have been better served had they listened to the Dave Hunts, et. al., whom God raised up to challenge the unscriptural revival they had participated in. Perhaps at least seriously considering Hunt's claims would have spared them from descending into the occult as they have.

The visit to the witch of Endor was the tragic "end of the road" for Saul, and I perceive that the slide into the occult is the sign of God's impending judgment on the "Prophetic movement." Didn't God warn us that He Himself would choose the delusions of those who refuse to "tremble at His Word"? Doesn't "judgment begin in the house of God"?

How did a movement which seemingly began out of a desire for more of God and His Spirit, end up with adherents reading auras, "soaking the anointing" from the graves of previous saints, and teaching dream interpretation at Christian conferences? (All of which are occult practices, forms of divination and abominable to God)!

Perhaps a recently released book, *The Physics of Heaven* can give us some insights as to how they got there. The book is a compendium of teachings by Bill Johnson, Larry Randolph, Bob Jones, and a few other notable NAR teachers and prophets compiled by Judy Franklin and Ellyn Davis.

From the introduction we are told that Franklin and Davis have assembled a "team of Christian seers" . . .

> In *The Physics of Heaven*, Judy Franklin and Ellyn Davis assemble a team of Christian seers who share their insights into how God is using sound, light, energy, vibrations, and the discoveries of quantum physics.

One of the first revelations confronting us in the book, is that a "Transformative Sound" is coming to the earth.

> Here is a prophetic word the Lord gave me about the coming importance of sound.
>
> Just as the people were in the upper room on the day of Pentecost, when suddenly there came from heaven an noise, and this noise was like a violent rushing wind, there will come again a noise that I will release from heaven. This noise, this sound, will be released and, just as those people in that upper room were changed, people who hear this sound that I will release will be changed.
>
> While I am not calling any of my people to sit in an upper room and wait, I am calling them to a place where their spirits are in an upper room position to receive what I am about to release. This sound that I will release will cause people to think differently.[1]

When God wants to transform people, He does it by presenting them the Word. He engages the mind, challenges them morally, intellectually and spiritually. He calls us to engage with Him on those levels. "Come, Let us reason together saith the Lord . . ."

One of the marks of occult or Gnostic models of personal transformation, is the fact that they aspire to antirational experience. People are zapped. They are slain in the Spirit or put into a trance. They might feel a presence, or in this case, the coming of a "transformative sound" is what will finally bring about change.

Bill Johnson himself testifies of this kind of irrational transformation in the testimony chapter of the book, "Whole Lotta Shakin Going On."

> In 1995 I began to cry out to God day and night for about 8 months. My prayer was "God I want more of you at any cost! I will pay any price!" Then one night in October, God came in answer to my prayer, but not in any way I had expected. I went from being in a dead sleep, to being wide awake in a moment. Unexplainable power began to surge through my body. If I had been plugged into a wall socket with a thousand volts going through my body, I can't imagine it would have been different. It was as though an extremely powerful being had entered the room and I couldn't function in his presence.[2]

Another "seer" relates a similar experience in the same chapter. Cal Pierce confessed that he was at a point in his life as a board member of an Assembly of God church of spiritual boredom. But one night in June of 1996, Bill Johnson laid hands on him and prayed.

> Without warning, I felt such a tremendous jolt of the power of God that my whole body began vibrating, as if an electric current was running through it, and I was shaking so hard I couldn't move. This lasted for hours, with me shaking and unable to move. When the shaking finally stopped, my life was completely changed . . .[3]

This is the Gnostic model of transformation—there is no Word, no thought engagement, no repentence (thinking again), no moral demands, just pure power!

But God has chosen to reveal His Son by the foolishness of preaching the gospel, thus engaging the mind, will, and yes emotions. This kind of engagement is what Gnostics and mystics are impatient with, relegating it to "dry doctrine," "mere head knowledge," and "yesterday's truth."

A MAN NAMED CAL Pierce says his life changed when he began to think and pray about the healing evangelist John G. Lake, from the early part of the last century. He prayed about him so much he went on a forty day fast and spent quite a bit of time visiting his grave . . . to pray. Eventually he opened up the John G. Lake "healing rooms" in Spokane, which had been closed for 80 years.

Does that not strike you as a little strange and even morbid? But many of those associated with Bill Johnson, and the NAR churches would have no problem with spending time in prayer at the grave of a deceased Christian.

Benny Hinn has long taught others the sin of necromancy.

Benny Hinn is just one Charismatic leader who has testified of his own necromancy (communication with the dead). He tells of his frequent visits to Kathryn Kuhlman's tomb, to get an impartation of "her anointing"!

> One of the strangest experiences I had a few years ago [was] visiting Aimee's tomb in California. This Thursday I'm on TBN. Friday I am gonna go and visit Kathryn Kuhlman's tomb. It's close by Aimee's in Forest Lawn Cemetery. I've been there once already and every so often I like to go and pay my respects 'cause this great woman of God has touched my life. And that grave, uh, where she's buried is closed, they built walls around it. You can't get in without a key and I'm one of the very few people who can get in. But I'll never forget when I saw Aimee's

tomb. It's incredibly dramatic. She was such a lady that her tomb has seven-foot angels bowing on each side of her tomb with a gold chain around it. As—as incredible as it is that someone would die with angels bowing on each side of her grave, I felt a terrific anointing when I was there. I actually, I—I, hear this, I trembled when I visited Aimee's tomb. I was shaking all over. God's power came all over me. . . . I believe the anointing has lingered over Aimee's body. I know this may be shocking to you. . . . And I'm going to take David [Palmquist] and Kent [Mattox] and Sheryl [Palmquist] this week. They're gonna come with me. You—you—you gonna feel the anointing at Aimee's tomb. It's incredible. And Kathryn's. It's amazing. I've heard of people healed when they visited that tomb. They were totally healed by God's power. You say, "What a crazy thing." Brother, there's things we'll never understand. Are you all hearing me?"[4].

Familiarity with the Word of God would deliver Hinn's followers, for God says He hates the sin of necromancy. Isaiah tells us that those who seek anything from the dead have no light in them.

When someone tells you to consult mediums and spiritists, who whisper and mutter, should not a people inquire of their God? Why consult the dead on behalf of the living? Consult God's instruction and the testimony of warning. If anyone does not speak according to this word, they have no light of dawn(Isaiah 8:9-12)

At his Bethel School of Ministry, Bill Johnson teaches students to "honor the generals of revival," that is, leaders such as Smith Wigglesworth, Aimee Semple McPherson, Evan Roberts, and others.

"Honoring" them to Johnson means compiling a vast collection of their books and artifacts, and opening a "generals library" for Charismatics to visit. But like Hinn, Johnson also believes in visiting their tombs, and literally "soaking" the "anointing" by being in the presence of their graves.[5]

ANOTHER REVEALING ASPECT OF *The Physics of Heaven* is the idea that we should entertain the possibility that New Agers could be onto something valid, and that we shouldn't throw out the baby with the bathwater. In the chapter called "Authentic versus Counterfeit," "seer" Jonathan Welton presents a fallacious thesis.

> If there is a counterfeit, there is an authentic that we need to find and reclaim. Every time we see a masquerade, we need to look closely to properly discern what is being counterfeited, because a counterfeit is evidence that an authentic exists.
>
> As Christians, when we see that Satan has created a counterfeit, we commonly overreact to try to protect ourselves from contamination. One way that we overreact is by throwing out anything that looks like the counterfeit, including the real. This is like burning all the money in your wallet because there are counterfeits in the world and deception is possible.[6]

Such reasoning sounds good but it isn't scriptural. We don't start with that which is false, in order to seek the truth. We have the Word of God. We needn't bother ourselves with the "deep things of Satan" to see if the pagans are incorrectly manifesting the power we should have but don't.

One of the ways these neo Gnostics deceive themselves and others, is by caricaturizing their critics. Those who object to mysticism within Christianity are "over reacting," afraid, and trying to "protect themselves." (It couldn't be that they are trying to be faithful to the Word of God could it?) In Welton's allegory above, those who eschew New Age mysticism are as foolish as one who would burn paper money!

This is the very reasoning which has seduced and deceived a whole generation of Christians into comfortably accepting what can only be regarded as occult Christianity. Here, Welton puts forth another familiar adage, designed to disarm discernment.

> Personally, I have a lot more faith in the Lord's ability to keep me than in the devil's ability to steal me away. Jesus said that He has us in His hand and no one can snatch us out. "I give them eternal life, and they shall never perish; no one can snatch them out of My hand" (John 10:28).

I too have faith in the Lord's ability and willingness to keep me, but because I have an equal respect for the Lord's warnings about deception in the last days, coupled with a profound distrust of my own capacity to remain faithful, I refuse to be cavalier about it.

This misguided and dangerous idea is taken further in the book, *The Physics of Heaven*. Jonathon Welton, in his chapter, "Authentic or Counterfeit," says,

> With all this talk about countefeit and authentic, by now you may be scratching your head hoping for examples. The best ones I have found are in the New Age movement. They have been trafficking in the church's stolen goods for a long time.I have found throughout scripture at least 75 examples of things the New Age has counterfeited, such as; having a spirit guide, trances, meditation, auras, power objects, clairvoyance, clairaudience, and more. These actually belong to the church, but they have been stolen and cleverly repackaged . . .

If the New Age Movement has had it right, (other than the part about Jesus being Lord), according to this kind of thinking, we should of course study the New Age teachings, so that we can "recover" the experiences and manifestations they have stolen from us, according to the authors and "Seers" of this book.

One of the co-authors, Ellyn Davis, reports that that is exactly what "the Lord" told her to do.

> In 2006, through God's inexplicable sense of humor, I found my self with an empty nest and a job offer in Sedona Arizona, the global epicenter of New Age thought and practice. By then I had experienced much of what charismatic Christianity has to offer, miracles, prophecy, healing, deep revelation, transformative experiences of the presence of the Holy Spirit, excellent Bible teaching, and I had been involved in at least five modern day moves of God in the church.
>
> I moved to Sedona fully prepared to discount everything I saw and heard as coming from another source other than the God I knew and loved. But as a scientist I was intrigued by what I had found there. I saw healings and mystical experiences, and revelations to rival anything I had seen or experienced in the church . . . It wasn't that I wanted to become a New Ager, I just wanted to find out if they had uncovered some truths the church had not, the strange thing was much of what I saw and heard embodied biblical principles and could be backed up by scripture.[7]

This is a serious defection from the Christianity of Jesus and the apostles. Never would Paul or Peter have commended pagans, Shamans, and occultists for having truths that the church could glean from. Peter told Simon the Great that he and his money were on the way to Hell.

The presupposition is that the church is just not walking in the power we could be, and that we must seek the reasons why, even if that search leads us to the New Age and the occult. After all, as the Pentecostal extremists used to say, "A man with an experience is never at the mercy of a man with mere doctrine."

Thus power is everything to these people. It is even more important than the truth, "once and for all revealed to the saints."

Davis was alone as far as she knew in her "discovery" that New Agers had truths that Christians don't currently possess, (but should). Unfortunately she reports

> At that time I could not find a single Christian leader who shared a similar interest in finding out if there were truths hidden in the New Age. Now we are beginning to hear more and more revelation that is in line with what New Agers have been saying all along . . .[8]

This is the blindness of those leading so many of God's professing people into the ditch. She and the seers she has compiled see it as a good thing that the Christian church has finally come around to some of the presuppositions of the New Age movement, which is nothing less than a a vicious enemy of the truth of the gospel.

Need I say more?

The extreme Charismatic church is in the same position as King Saul was—backslidden, blinded, stumbling in the dark, and deeply involved in the very occult she once vigorously decried.

13

Why God Holds Pastors Responsible

A wonderful and horrible thing is committed in the land;
The prophets prophesy falsely, and the priests bear rule
by their means; and my people love to have it so: and
what will ye do in the end thereof? (Jeremiah 5:30-31).

I think you'll find that the prophets are pretty nice
people, by and large. I've come to know them and love
them. We've invited several of them here, I think maybe
five or six, that are from the Kansas City Fellowship. And
then we have Paul Cain . . .[1]

JEREMIAH 23 IS A polemic against false prophets, which starts out
by putting the blame where it really belongs. Who does the Lord
initially make responsible for the explosion of false prophets? Not
the false prophets, nor the congregations, but the pastors! God
knows that the ministries of these false prophets would be all but
impossible without pastors opening up their platforms and pulpits
to them. The judgment of God upon these is certain, as God says
in His Word:

Woe be unto the pastors that destroy and scatter the
sheep of my pasture! saith the Lord.

> Therefore thus saith the LORD God of Israel against
> the pastors that feed my people; Ye have scattered my
> flock, and driven them away, and have not visited them:
> behold, I will visit upon you the evil of your doings, saith
> the LORD. (Jeremiah 23:1-2)

How would these false prophets even exist without shepherds opening up their pulpits to give them meetings? Therefore it is the shepherds that God addresses when He opens up this passage about false prophets. Pastors are supposed to feed their sheep the Word of God, and protect them from wolves. The flourishing of false prophets is an indictment against we who are pastors for failing to faithfully do this. The Word of God, like manna, has failed to satisfy the lust too many have for the novel and exciting. A good number of shepherds are going to have to answer to charges that for gain, and out of greed, or fear of being left out, we have opened our flocks to the teachings and prophecies of these men who speak such great swelling words of vanity.

The current false movements have succeeded in creating an incredible peer pressure in the ministry. The pressure is on to distinguish oneself as the leader of a church which is "cutting edge," spot-on with the latest religious fads. The last thing anyone would want to be accused of is being "dead" or "religious." Thus a good many pastors are "desperate"; but it is not the desperation that pushes an individual to seek God. These days it is a rampant emotionalism that fuels the kind of desperation many pastors are experiencing, spurring them to keep up with the fast-moving trends in the religious world of today. Often, a pastor's motivation for "church growth" is rooted in envy at the church down the road, or, from a more mercenary standpoint, fear that if his people leave due to his reluctance to partake of the latest revival, he would find himself out of a job. For all the talk about "surrendering all" for Jesus, many pastors unfortunately have the bottom line as the dollar sign. It is morbidly fascinating that this kind of desperation rarely seems to invite fasting and prayer; rather, it provokes a visceral fear that manifests itself in conferences and church-growth seminars.

One pastor was asked why, in spite of his admitted reservations, he plunged his church into the now-defunct Toronto Blessing. His candid reply speaks volumes about the state of many in church leadership today:

> I wasn't sure if it was of God or not, but we were so dry, and so desperate we couldn't afford not to take the chance . . .

Results. Truth is secondary these days. So many pastors toss aside sound doctrine, and hence, protection for their flocks, with a flippant, "Just give us some results, generate some excitement, or we will scatter in this wilderness." Sounds much like the attitude of the children of Israel as they repeatedly grumbled to Moses. Even in their forty-year wilderness wanderings the Israelites saw the mighty hand of God bring water out of a rock, send bread from heaven itself, and destroy formidable armies that came against them. Each and every moment they could see their God go before them as a pillar of cloud by day and a pillar of fire by night. But it never seemed enough. So sold were they on the validity of their carnal grievances that they believed their way was better than God's, that He had somehow short-changed them and they were compelled to make up the difference. Many pastors today are following their lead.

Hirelings are defined as those who run, when the wolf comes, rather than lay down their lives to protect God's sheep. Who are the modern hirelings? They are the ones who know that these new religious fads are unscriptural, but are afraid of standing up to them, lest they lose their numbers, prestige, "anointed" reputation, and so forth. Like Aaron in the golden calf incident, they know this is wrong, but in order not to scatter the people, they are willing to offer them something to see, feel, and experience. They don't openly or knowingly advocate a new God, but they inaugurate ways of worshiping Him, and "points of contact" to Him that He Himself has never instituted. This is called "will worship" in the King James Version of the Scriptures, and it means "the worship of God on our own terms." As in the golden calf incident in the Book of Exodus, these new prophets have proclaimed a "feast unto Jahweh" where there is no feast! (Exodus 32:5).

There are a lot of Aarons these days in Pentecostal and Charismatic leadership, who know that these movements—like the Toronto Blessing, the Brownsville Revival, Promise Keepers, drunkenness in the spirit and holy laughter, ecumenism, etc.—are wrong. But they are afraid of losing their lives and ministries for truth, so they compromise. Besides it has always been profitable, if even short-term, to cater to the latest religious fads. When Aaron took an offering for the golden calf, it was one of the most willing offerings ever taken, for it is just fallen human nature for people to gladly pay for the idols of their preference.

> And Aaron said unto them, Break off the golden earrings, which are in the ears of your wives, of your sons, and of your daughters, and bring them unto me. And all the people brake off the golden earrings which were in their ears, and brought them unto Aaron (Exodus 32:2-3).

The actions of the Assemblies of God are a vivid example of this, for that group condemned both Toronto and the laughing revival, until they had their own version of it. What is the difference between Toronto and Pensacola? One gave birth to the other. Pensacola sprang from the Holy Trinity Brompton Church in London, England. HTB was the church which virtually blanketed England with the Toronto Blessing, and which literally coined the phrase, "Toronto Blessing." Can both good and bad water come from the same source (James 3:11)? (see Appendix 2).

How the Assemblies of God could have shone brightly these days, holding up the truth of the Gospel! There are many independent Pentecostals who have looked up to the Assemblies, because of their previous strength, experience, and holiness. I have no doubt that there are still many within the denomination who are grieved over the apostasy, but the leadership seems to have taken the "ends justify the means" approach. These new revivals are appealing because they do generate excitement! It is because of the hireling mentality of the shepherds, the pastors, that the people of God were affected by the prophets. And what are those effects?

Folly and Error

And I have seen folly in the prophets of Samaria . . . [they] caused my people Israel to err (Jeremiah 23:13).

THERE ARE NUMEROUS EXAMPLES of the folly and error that false prophets have brought upon God's people. Jacob Prasch tells of the British prophet Gerald Coates (see Appendix 3), who foretold an earthquake in New Zealand. This prophecy persuaded the leaders of a Pentecostal denomination to appear on national television to warn the nation. The national news coverage leading up to it featured churches taking survival courses, on the basis of that prophetic "word." When the predicted date came and went without fanfare, the Christian church was made into a national laughing-stock. A sincere, but naive Christian leader was made a fool of in his own nation, all because he allowed himself and many to listen to a false prophet's predictions.

It's interesting to note that, these days, we hear little of these failed prophecies. And make no mistake—the failure of Coates's prophecy was epic. While it's a horrible enough sin to give a false "word" to an individual, it is magnified a hundred-fold when spread out to encompass an entire nation. The fear generated among sincere believers, the wild scurry to procure extra rations of food, medical supplies, etc., and the pleading with unsaved loved ones to prepare for a national disaster that never happened likely left a faith wreckage in its wake. How many genuine Christian men and women exited their church groups, perhaps with bitterness, in the aftermath? For some it may have been the last straw. Tired of weathering the mockery of unbelievers, some may have determined that they would never again darken the doorway of a church.

The above is a point that needs to be repeatedly stressed. By and large, the new prophets appear to take little to no responsibility for their failures. It seems of little consequence to them that they have, at a minimum, disrupted lives, or, at worst, are responsible for the shipwrecked faith of many. It is a grave thing to speak in the name of the Lord. Well Jesus speaks to them today when He said, "But I say unto you, that every idle word that men shall speak, they shall give account thereof in the day of judgment. For by thy words thou shalt be justified, and by thy words thou shalt be condemned" (Matthew 12:36-37).

Profaneness

> . . . for from the prophets of Jerusalem is profaneness gone forth into all the land (Jeremiah 23:15).

Do you know what the word "profaneness" means? To profane something means to make it into something common, nothing special at all. It is the opposite of the words "holy," or "sacred," both of which mean special, set apart. God's Word is holy, special and set apart. It is to be regarded as holy by His people. When Christians, who have been bought with the blood of the Lamb, and have received the Holy Spirit, and been exposed to the Bible feel they then need to go out, crossing land and sea, to get a "word from the Lord," through people like the Kansas City Prophets, they are profaning the holy Word of God.

The Word of God is being profaned by those who are constantly saying things like, "God is a lot more than God the Father, God the Son, and God the Holy Book" or "God is a lot bigger than a doctrine" or even "The church is so hung up on 'bible study' that they don't really know Jesus." These are the same people who produce reams and reams of prophecies, expecting you to take those seriously! This profanity will spill out into other areas for it cannot long be contained. I believe that the prophecy movement is partly responsible for a kind of "been-there-done-that" attitude to the teaching and preaching of the Word of God.

They Make You Vain!

> Thus saith the LORD of Hosts, Hearken not to the words of the prophets that prophesy unto you: they make you vain: they speak a vision of their own heart, and not out of the mouth of the LORD (Jeremiah 23:16).

THE FALSE PROPHETS WILL make you vain! This is the warning of Jeremiah, to those who would be enamored of these new seers. In biblical thought, vanity is a blight to be avoided, for it means "lightness,"" "irrelevancy," "to be futile and of no consequence."

Think about it; we live in a world that is in spiritual and moral confusion, and a good many thinking people are aware of this, both saved and unsaved. At a time when the Christian church could be holding forth substantial answers, biblical responses that actually speak to the current dilemma of man, and answers that are a part of our inheritance from Christ, we are instead being seduced into abandonment of our thinking faculties. The Rodney Howard Brownes of this world beckon us to "turn off your mind and go with the flow." This is the same form of spirituality practiced in much of the New Age mysticism.

This false prophetic movement has made us vain! It has promised renewal to countless thousands of pastors and churches, but instead has promoted a God-dishonoring self aggrandizement. That shouldn't surprise us when we consider the content of the bulk of these prophecies. They are generally of the "You-are-the-greatest-generation-of-the-church-ever" variety, or they club compliance out of Christians with the Annanias and Sapphira threat of God's impending judgment on those who question or resist "this move of

God." After twenty years or more of either wielding this immense power over people, or being the recipient of congratulatory prophecies, anyone would be vain. Pastors, we are responsible for this. Why have we opened the flocks up to this spiritual abuse? What were we looking for when we sought these ministries? We have succeeded in making our people vain, when they could be sharp, sober and ready, able to give an answer for the hope we have in Christ, instead of being self absorbed, drunk in the spirit, living for the next "outpouring."

I warned in my earlier book, *Weighed and Found Wanting: Putting the Toronto Blessing in Context*, that spiritual drunkenness is real, but it is not a blessing from God. It is, rather, a judgment on an unfaithful and unbelieving church! Isaiah proclaims:

> His watchmen are blind: they are all ignorant, they are all dumb dogs, they cannot bark; sleeping, lying down, loving to slumber, Yea, they are greedy dogs which can never have enough, and they are shepherds that cannot understand: they all look to their own way, everyone for his gain, from his quarter. Come ye, say they, I will fetch wine and we willfi ll ourselves with strong drink; and tomorrow shall be as this , and much more abundant. (Isaiah 56:10-12)

They Encourage Those Who Despise the Lord

> They say still unto them that despise me, The LORD hath said, Ye shall have peace; and they say unto every one that walketh in the imagination of his own heart, No evil shall come upon you (Jeremiah 23:17).

THERE IS A TREMENDOUS judgment coming upon our nation for her many sins, and of course judgment must begin in the house of God, for as Peter has rightly said, "And if the righteous scarcely be saved, where shall the ungodly and the sinner appear?" (1

Peter 4:18). Peter and the apostles called the church to soberness, vigilance, good works, and so forth in view of the coming day of God's judgment. He could not be plainer when he wrote,

> Seeing then that all these things shall be dissolved, what manner of persons ought ye to be in all holy conversation and godliness. Looking for and hasting unto the coming of the day of God . . . (2 Peter 3:11-12).

Those who despise the Lord are not necessarily those who hate the Lord, for in biblical usage, to despise is to esteem lightly, to fail to take a person seriously. The new prophets are dangerous, because they make the church the issue and not the Lord. Their prophecies, as I have already demonstrated, are about the coming greatness of the church, what we will do, how we will reign, and our exploits (of course, "in the power of God"). The actual bodily return of Jesus is not the true goal of the new prophets. In many cases, rather, it is the coming glory, the "presence of God" that has been prophesied by these to envelope the church in the days immediately preceding the bodily return of Jesus. Instead of calling men to "Fear God, and give glory to Him, for the hour of His judgment is come" (Revelation 14:7), a self-indulgent church is being urged to "soak" up as much of the "anointing" as possible, to get drunk on the New Wine, and to enlist themselves into Joel's Army, an army that itself is doomed to be judged by God! (Joel 2:20).

They encourage those who despise the Lord to carry on in a thousand and one ways! For example, if a man really fears the Lord, he will want to exercise discernment, to think critically, and to not just throw open his spirit to every passing religious fad. These new prophets strongly discourage this, to the point of mockery and threatening! They have helped foster an antagonism in the church between the ones whom they have seduced, and those who are more cautious. The "Civil War" prophecy of Joyner, Campbell, Bob Jones, and James Ryle, the sarcasm of Rodney

Howard-Browne (rarely missing an opportunity to mock and castigate his detractors), and the whole "us/them" mentality has given much encouragement to those who despise the Lord enough to relish this division. What the prophet Jeremiah wrote thousands of years ago could have been penned just this morning:

> But if they had stood in my council and had caused my people to hear my words, then they should have turned them from their evil way, and from the evil of their doings (Jeremiah 23:22).

In conclusion, the pastors have been given the charge to feed and protect the flock of God, which He purchased with His own Blood. Therefore, the responsibility for the false prophets in part is laid to rest at their feet. These false prophets would not be able to operate if the people of God had been fed sound doctrine, and if the shepherds were willing to wield their protective staves as the Lord commands. Therefore the chapter in Jeremiah that explicitly discusses false prophets, begins with, "Woe be unto the Pastors . . . " (Jeremiah 23:1). In the very face of false predictions, outrageous teaching and operating in counterfeit spiritual gifts, too many pastors insist that all of that can be overlooked for the potential benefits that these false prophets offer.

14

The Distinguishing Marks of a False Prophet

We should not judge Bill Clinton solely by how he may appear at this time. We cannot continue to get our discernment from the news Media. The Bill Clinton that the Lord showed Paul Cain in the dream is different from the media's portrayal of him. We must start to see people as the Lord sees them . . . Bill Clinton won and so can we. The reason Paul Cain was shown five headlines in the dream is because Bill Clinton represents grace from God, not judgment . . .[1]

Error, indeed, is never set forth in its naked deformity, lest it being thus exposed, it should at once be detected. But it is craftily decked out in an attractive dress, so as, by its outward form, to make it appear to the inexperienced . . . more true than the truth itself.[2]

THE TIME HAS COME for the practical portion of this book. Our burden from the start, has been to provide the believer with the necessary equipment for the exercise of discernment in these times—specially for the pastors, who must contend with this swelling tide of error. We are reminded of two assurances from our merciful Lord, that "When the enemy shall come in like a flood, the Spirit of the LORD shall lift up a standard against him" (Isaiah

59:19), and also we are told that by the knowledge of the Holy Scriptures, "The man of God may be perfect, thoroughly furnished unto all good works" (2 Timothy 3:17). With those thoughts in mind, let us take a look at what the Word of God sets forth as the distinguishing marks of false prophets.

False Prophets Make False Predictions

THE FOUNDATIONAL TEST IS laid out by Moses, and it is quite simple: predictions made by false prophets don't come to pass.

> And if thou say in thine heart, How shall we know the word which the Lord hath not spoken? When a prophet speaketh in the name of the LORD, if the thing follow not, nor come to pass, that is the thing which the Lord hath not spoken, but the prophet hath spoken presumptuously: thou shalt not be afraid of Him. (Deuteronomy 18:21-22)

It is truly amazing to me that this simple prescription, given for the safety of God's people, is considered inapplicable, on the basis of it being Old Testament teaching. Nowhere in the New Testament is this simple test invalidated. We are never counseled by Jesus or the apostles to consider in any sense that those who make inaccurate predictions are to be accepted as prophets of God.

Much of the current confusion we are seeing these days on this point is a result of the inability to distinguish three separate functions of prophetic grace. There are first the Old Testament prophets, then New Testament prophets, and finally those used in the utterance gifts of the Spirit.

All basically agree that the Old Testament prophets, such as Isaiah, Jeremiah, and Ezekiel, fall under the Deuteronomy 18 test. Not one Old Testament prophet could be inaccurate, not even in 1% of their prophetic utterances!

Concerning the third category. Those used in the utterance

gifts of the Spirit—prophesying for "edification, exhortation, and comfort" (1 Corinthians 14:3)—are not in the same category as those who call themselves prophets. Any Christian may potentially be given a prophetic utterance (1 Corinthians 14:31). But to be used in that gift is not the same as being a prophet. Acts 21:9-10 brings out this distinction.

> And the same man had four daughters, virgins, which did prophesy. And as we tarried there many days, there came down from Judea a certain prophet, named Agabus.

The new prophets don't claim to merely give prophecies; rather they insist that they are "moving in a prophetic anointing." They supposedly have conversations with angels, God, and demons. They dream interactive dreams, and make proclamations in the name of the Lord. Some have claimed they've taken a round trip to heaven!

As for their pronouncements, they make them to the whole church. In reality, they consider themselves prophets in the sense of Isaiah and Jeremiah, which case they should be willing to submit to the same test, for the church's sake.

As we have already demonstrated, the contention is that inaccuracy is allowed in New Testament times, because, you know, "immature," prophets are allowed now to "develop" their gifts! It amounts to an almost evolutionary view of prophets, men and women who are still "growing into 100% accuracy."

Much is made of 1 Corinthians 14:29, "Let the prophets speak two or three, and let the others judge." This passage is simply telling us that prophecy is to be judged. Paul is saying the same thing that Moses says in Deuteronomy chapters 13 and 18. The difference now is that the church is not a theocratic nation-state as was Israel, and it has no option of capital punishment. Fortunately for some, we don't stone false prophets. On the other hand, neither is there any indication that we should allow the ministry of inaccurate prophets to be received. The penalty for false prophecy has lessened in a temporal sense, but the seriousness of it hasn't.

We can see in the Book of Acts that there were New Testament prophets, who seemed to operate in the same sense as the Old Testament prophets. Obviously, Agabus is one example. It is helpful to note that his prophecies were always validated by God. I have yet to be shown even one New Testament prophet who made inaccurate prophecies!

As for the prophets we have dealt with in this book, the inaccuracies made in the name of the Lord are numerous! We have already mentioned the much heralded prophecy that "all evil would be ripped off of the face of the earth on June 9, 1994," a date which came and went without much stir. In early 1993, Rick Joyner and Paul Cain both had optimistic things to say about Bill Clinton. Cain was shown five headlines in a dream, because, five is the number of grace. As he said,

> Bill Clinton represents grace from God, not judgment . . .
> In the dream Paul was told that Bill Clinton was better than what we deserved, and that he may be viewed as the best president in America since Dwight Eisenhower . . .
> The Lord wants to use Bill Clinton to move the country forward and not backward.[3]

Here we are, these many years later, and the country has gone from bad to worse.

The same Spirit told Cain and Joyner that Clinton represents a "Reprieve from a New World Order that the church is not prepared to face at this time." The whole Clinton presidency was nothing but an advancement of the policies of the New World Order! This prediction has failed to come to pass, putting the validity of these "prophets" in question.

For all the great things these new prophets utter about America and the church here, we need to look at cold, hard facts. The nation is spiraling ever downward, spiritually. Christians are being targeted as "intolerant" and "hate mongers," and many of the policies that have gone forth from both congress and the White House have proven antithetical to the very faith of Christ.

Hey, is that a good prophetic record or what?

Any thinking individual can clearly see that the spirit that moves these prophets is not the Holy Spirit. Can any mature believer accept that God actually gives false prophecies to His prophets, because the true, unadulterated Word of God would result in too many Annaniases and Sapphiras? That God actually loads the "gun" of the prophet with "blanks"? Have we, as a church, sunk into such spiritual lethargy that common sense is now regarded an enemy of Christ?

May God have mercy on us.

False Prophets Have False Doctrine

WHEN CONSIDERING ANY PROPHETS, we have to not allow ourselves to be sidetracked by the miracles, signs and wonders, and even the predictions, for none of these are central to the essence of prophetic ministry. All prophets, true or false, bring a message. The signs and wonders (if there are any) only serve to validate that message; they are not ends in themselves! Remember, the greatest prophet ever born of woman, as Jesus said of John the Baptist, did no miracles! Signs and wonders and predictions are not essential to prophetic ministry, but the message of the prophet is.

Isaiah and Jeremiah didn't go around giving people personal "words" at meetings! Neither did John the Baptist nor Agabus. Moses didn't throw his cloak at crowds to see them slain in the spirit. These godly men were first of all preachers and teachers. In the process of giving their messages, which called Israel back to the Law of Moses and the nations to God in repentance, and warned both of coming judgments, they did indeed often make predictions, and effect healings. But what they were truly about was what they referred to as "their burden," "the Word of the Lord" which came to them. Their text was the Holy Scripture.

This is why Moses warned us in Deuteronomy 13, and John in 1 John chapter 4, that when "testing the spirits" of prophets or ministries, it is not enough to know that so-and-so was healed, or that this-or-that family was brought together, for even the Mormons have produced that much. The true issue is always, "What is the content of the message?" If prophets are preachers and teachers, it follows that false prophets are false teachers! Peter makes this connection in 2 Peter 2:1when he writes,

> But there were false prophets also among the people, even as there shall be false teachers among you, who privily shall bring in damnable heresies, even denying the Lord that bought them, and bring upon themselves swift destruction.

The thought conveyed in the Greek is that they shall subtly lay lies alongside of truth in such a way that the two are all but indistinguishable. There are many "good" things being said by many of these teachers and preachers. But we have to remember that rat poison is 95% nutritious!

This is why Jesus told us in Matthew 12:35-37 that the fruit of a prophet, is his words. "For by thy words thou shalt be justified, and by thy words thou shalt be condemned." This is no different from Moses' warning of the prophet or dreamer of dreams, whose prediction may well have appeared to come to pass, but whose consistent message is a form of "let us go after other gods, which thou hast not known, and let us serve them," or John's warning, that "every spirit that confesseth not that Jesus Christ is come in the flesh is not of God: and this is that spirit of antichrist . . ." All are agreed that the test of a prophet is his or her doctrine. False prophets are off because their doctrines are off. Of these there are myriad examples. Jewel Van Der Merwe recounts one such example in her *Discernment Newsletter* of March 1993, when she writes:

On February 25, 1993, a "prophet" was on TBN with

Matt Crouch, the son of Paul and Jan . . . On this particular broadcast it was taught that the Body of Christ doesn't understand what the prophet really is. They just don't understand that the Old Testament prophet was different from the New Testament prophet. Naturally they would say that! . . . the way a prophet is defined today makes him not responsible for his prophecies! All the responsibility falls upon the person to whom the prophecy is given! If the prophecy doesn't come to pass, it is that person's fault . . . The new prophets are claiming their utterances are . . . literally the UTTERANCE OF GOD . . . the "spoken Word" . . . the "Fresh Word from God." This word is on a par with, and in some instances above the written Word. Their claim is that the "spoken word" actually makes the "prophet" a partaker of the DIVINE NATURE . . . On the TBN program, this particular "prophet" Kim Clement, actually said that the Christians will be a superhuman powerful force that will grind Satan into the ground. The very topping on the cake was that the Word of God when used was twisted. For example, Matthew 16:16-18, "Peter . . . said, Thou art Christ, the Son of the Living God. And Jesus . . . said . . . flesh and blood has not revealed it unto thee, but my Father which is in heaven . . . and upon this rock I will build my church; and the gates of Hell will not prevail against it." . . . This scripture was interpreted on this program as meaning, "Christians must get into revelation from the Word." Yes this sounds very good. However it is how "the Word" is defined that is so troubling. By the "Word," this "prophet" means a fresh prophetic voice, or revelation experienced subjectively apart from the literal Bible revelation. He intimated that for Christians to survive they must build on new subjective revelations and experiences. This concept makes the written Word of God of no effect, especially if this new revelation is put on a par with scripture . . . So the Prophet continues ". . . and upon this rock of revelation, I will build my church. There has to be a fresh revelation for the church today to build on, and the Gates of Hell will not prevail against the rock of this fresh revelation!" . . . Matt Crouch's enthusiastic response was, "The Word that we heard as children is not fresh revelation and is not applicable for today. It isn't any good for the warfare today . . . we are building on Christ and Fresh revelation."[4]

If Matt Crouch "got it," so did the thousands of television viewers who happened to be tuned in that day to receive ministry from the TBN prophet. But what did they "get"? They seemed to be getting the same thing that Eve got when she listened to that long, skinny prophet, coiled around the tree of the knowledge of good and evil. "Has God said?" In other words, "The Word that we heard as children is not fresh . . . no longer applicable for today." No amount of accurate predictions, conversions, healings or apparent miracles should induce a child of God to accept such a ministry, after hearing that kind of teaching.

False Prophets Hate to Be Tested

JEREMIAH WAS A TRUE prophet, who ministered in the final days of the kingdom of Judah, immediately before the Babylonian captivity. Another prophet named Hananiah, was far more popular in the land of Judah. His name means "God has been gracious." Names can be deceiving. False prophets usually come across as gracious and humble, initially, but sooner or later, their dark side comes out.

God had instructed Jeremiah to wear a yoke of bondage, as a sign of the coming captivity. Hananiah came forth with an utterance to Jeremiah in the temple, in front of all of the priests and people. He said:

Thus speaketh the LORD of Hosts, the God of Israel

> saying, I have broken the yoke of the king of Babylon.
> Within two full years will I bring again into this place
> all the vessels of the LORD's house (Jeremiah 28:2-3).

Hananiah prophesied the opposite of what Jeremiah the prophet had been warning of, in the temple, in the presence of the priests! Jeremiah's response was that he would love for Hananiah's prophecy to be true, but it was in contradiction to all of the previous prophets, to prophesy SHALOM (Peace, all is well) when the nation was sinful and unrepentant. At this point Hananiah suddenly lost his gracious and humble composure, for he walked up to Jeremiah, took off of him the yoke that the LORD had told him to wear, and broke it!

> Then said the prophet Jeremiah unto Hananiah the prophet, Hear now Hananiah; The LORD hath not sent thee, but thou makest this people to trust in a lie. Therefore thus saith the LORD ; Behold, I will cast thee off from the face of the earth: this year thous shalt die, because thous hast taught rebellion against the LORD (Jeremiah 28:15-16).

True prophets don't mind scrutiny, as long as they are being measured by the standard of the Word of God. False prophets resent it and castigate those who would dare appeal to the standard of judgment as being "religious," judgmental, "fearful," and reactionary. Those who refuse to exercise discernment are applauded as being "open to God."

False Prophets Are Man Centered

> Woe unto you when all men shall speak well of you! for so did their fathers to the false prophets . . . (Luke 6:26)

As Jewel Van Der Merwe notes:

[P]ositive prophecies also came out on the TBN program with Kim Clement and Matt Crouch. Kim said he was tired of "so-called prophets" saying that this country was going to be judged. He didn't think this country would be judged because they send out so many missionaries. Instead, he believed that tremendous blessing was coming on America. In fact, he stated that the body of Christ is becoming very aggressive, songs becoming militant, and the church is getting ready to fight. In fact if you prophesy "doom and gloom" you are not going to be a part of what God is going to do! He was prophesying that there is going to be an incredible breakthrough and revival in twenty months.[5]

Kim Clement is a man widely acclaimed as a prophet. A full-page ad in *Charisma Magazine* heralded his meetings in Detroit, with the announcement, "The Light has come to Detroit!" Who wouldn't want incredible blessing to come upon America? Peter and Jude both warn of those who would come along speaking "great swelling words, having men's persons in admiration because of advantage" (Jude 16).

False Prophets Can Be Accurate in Their Signs

JUST BECAUSE A PROPHET has a few miracles in his ministry doesn't mean he is of God. Mormonism began with the working of a number of apparent miracles. Roman Catholicism has its miracles also. The Word of God warns us that in the last days the truth will be withstood by men like Jannes and Jambres.

> Now as Jannes and Jambres withstood Moses, so do these also resist the truth: men of corrupt minds, reprobate concerning the faith (2 Timothy 3:8).

Jannes and Jambres were the prophets who stood before Pharaoh, and seemed to have "the stuff" in the days of Moses.

Up to a point, they could virtually duplicate all of the miracles of Moses. Paul warns us of the time in the last days, when the truth will be resisted by similar miracle workers. He said in another place, that we should be aware of the coming of him "whose coming is after the working of satan, with all power and signs and lying wonders, and with all deceivableness of unrighteousness in them that perish; because they received not the love of the truth, that they might be saved. And for this cause God shall send them strong delusion, that they should believe a lie . . ." (2 Thessalonians 2:9-11).

It is hard for modern people to imagine that God Himself would actually "send strong delusion" upon us in the last days. This is admittedly a hard word. But Paul is saying in a New Testament context what Moses had already told us when he wrote,

> If there arise among you a prophet, or a dreamer of dreams, and giveth thee a sign or a wonder, and the sign or wonder come to pass, whereof he spake unto thee saying, Let us go after other gods, which thou hast not known, and let us serve them; Thou shalt not hearken unto the words of that prophet, or that dreamer of dreams, for the LORD your God proveth you, to know whether ye love the Lord your God with all your heart and all your soul (Deuteronomy 13:13).

Therefore we can conclude that it is the Lord who allows false prophets to flourish at times, and even allows their signs to seem valid! And why does He allow this? That He might prove our love. Do we love the Lord our God? On a subjective basis, I am convinced that there has never been a time in the history of Western civilization, where more people felt as though they were passionately in love with God. Never have the songs of praise and adoration and worship, been so intensely emotional, intimate, almost romantic! People are swooning for God, young people are getting drunk in the spirit for God, and love for God is provoking people to literally abandon all of their thinking faculties in the pursuit of passion for God.

But how does God say we should love Him? The Word of God makes reference to "will worship" in Colossians 2:23. Will worship refers, not to the worship of the will, but to the worship of God according to the human will. God tells us not only to love Him, but even how He is to be loved. What does it mean to love God? How does God define loving God?

The rise of false prophets forces us to confront this issue in our own lives, because to God, love translates into loyalty. If you love God, then you will be willing to judge and discern prophets, rejecting the ones who bring a false message, in spite of any apparent signs or wonders. All those who follow the people we have mentioned in this book, are undoubtedly sure that they "love God"! But to God, the proof of that love is shown when miracle working, signs and wonders dealing false prophets arise. Loyalty to God is loyalty to the revealed Word of God. Jesus said, "If you love me you will keep my Word."

We are on the verge of the greatest test any of us have ever been involved in. The steady stream of false Christian ministries have conditioned many of us to accept almost anybody who comes in the name of the Lord. If Christians will accept uncritically the outrageous teachings of a Benny Hinn or a Rodney Howard Browne, what will we do when a demonically inspired deceiver like the Antichrist comes along? If we can't see through Robert Schuller, the Pope or Mother Teresa, how are we going to withstand the ultimate false prophet of Revelation 13?

Those who are faithful in little will be given more, and in the last days, what is going to be given to the faithful, is understanding. As Daniel, a real prophet of God said,

> And such as do wickedly against the covenant shall he corrupt by flatteries: But the people that do know their God shall be strong and do exploits, And they that

understand among the people shall instruct many . . . (Daniel 11:32-33).

Amid all the turmoil of the current spiritual decay, we have a promise that will anchor our hearts no matter the storm.

> Now unto Him that is able to keep you from falling, and to present you faultless before the presence of His glory with exceeding joy, to the only wise God our Saviour, be glory and majesty, dominion and power, both now and ever. Amen (Jude 24-25).

Grow in Grace.

15

On the Verge? . . . But of What?

QUO VADIS? WHERE ARE we going? We, being the Pentecostal and Charismatic movement, and even the Evangelical church of Jesus Christ. There are those who say that we are on the verge of the "greatest revival the church has ever known." They confidently assert that the Toronto and Pensacola revivals were on the forefront of the long awaited and much prophesied, "last days, worldwide revival" that is to sweep whole nations into the Kingdom of God and cause the names of modern prophets and apostles to become known worldwide. "Nations will tremble at the mention of their name," is how one modern-day prophet described it.

On the other hand, there are those who see current trends in a more ominous light. Rather than a great last days revival, many are beginning to ask the question that Jesus posed in Luke 18:8—"When the Son of man cometh, shall he find faith on the earth?" Thus there is a polarization, a parting of the ways among Christians who are equally sincere in their beliefs.

Where are we going? Revival or apostasy? I believe that the Gospel of Matthew has something to say to these times in the form of two sayings of the Lord Jesus, who spoke of these in the context of discussion about the last days and the professing church. These statements seem to point to a progression of error, resulting in the apostasy of many.

They Will Say to Me, Lord, Lord . . .

THE FIRST STEP IN the progression is what I will refer to as an easy believism, a cheapened view of salvation. In Matthew 7: 21-23, Jesus exposes this false belief system. "Lord, Lord, . . ." will be the cry of many! In other words, Christianity will be "in." In some way, it will be popular with the masses. And, of course, I think all will agree that we have succeeded in popularizing Christianity to the point where everyone seems to be wearing crosses, Christian artists are being accepted in secular markets, and prominent athletes testify publically of conversion experiences. Even the President of the United States seems as comfortable in a church as in the corridors of power. In one sense, it seems that Evangelical Christians have actually succeeded in Christianizing the nation on every level. Thousands of us are saying, "Lord, Lord, . . ." We know the songs, read the books and partake of the popular Christian culture. Christianity is "in." It's made it. I remember the election of 1976 when Jimmy Carter announced that he was a "born again" Christian and the media didn't know what that even meant! A few short decades later and the words "born again" are mainstream, immediately understood by most Western people.

But what kind of Christianity have these thousands embraced? Are we as Christian as we think we are? If so, many thousands have been "born again." How, then, do we explain the wholesale degeneration of our society? There is nothing wrong with saying "Lord, Lord, . . ." and singing of the Lord and praying to the Lord, as long as He truly has been acknowledged as LORD, the Master, and King! But, the first warning of Jesus in these seven warnings is the warning of false conversion.

There are many who would swear up and down that they are saved, born again, that they prayed a prayer and asked Jesus to be their "personal Savior," who aren't actually saved. They will be shocked on that Day, that their confidence was misplaced. "Depart from Me, ye that work iniquity." In other words, "You did your own thing!" Iniquity, or lawlessness, is the blight of our day, the prevalent sin of our time. And somehow or other, we have reshaped our presentation of the gospel to lead many to believe that there can be a salvation for those who don't really want to obey the Lord, but want fire insurance.

The antidote to this is to look again at the sermons of the Book of Acts. The issues that the apostles addressed in their evangelism were not the same ones we press these days. We talk often to sinners about the love of Jesus, and the "wonderful plan" God has for their lives. We imply that God is out there waiting for them to just "open up" to Him so that He, also, can be a part of their life. Sinners imagine that when they are ready, they can "invite Jesus to be their personal Savior." Small wonder the churches are full of religious consumers, Christians on their own terms who have never imagined that they have to fear God. Not so the evangelism of the Book of Acts! The issues that the apostles emphasized were different; the point never was to "invite Jesus to be your personal Savior," nor even to "make Jesus your Lord." How can sinful man "make Jesus Lord?" As Peter proclaimed in Acts 2:36, "God hath made that same Jesus, whom ye have crucified, both Lord and Christ." Jesus is Lord, and God commands you to recognize this! Law, the broken law of God, was discussed first, not love. No one invited Jesus to come in. They were commanded to turn to Him while there was still time. There was none of this, "He'll always be there waiting for you," nonsense. Instead, the message preached was always "Save yourself from this perverted generation!" Jude tells us that "of some have compassion, making a difference," but others must be saved ". . . with fear, pulling them out of the fire; hating even the garment spotted by the flesh."

Nonetheless, many say unto Him, "Lord, Lord, . . ." and are totally unaware of their great danger. But our progression doesn't stay here, it moves on . . .

Didn't We Prophesy In Thy Name?

FALSE CHRISTIANS NEED TO be entertained and, like the Israelites becoming bored with manna, soon feel that the Bible gets, well, old, predictable and boring. For those who have heard all the sermons, over and over again, and yet still yearn for a "Word from the Lord," there has arisen a Prophetic movement, which we have attempted to document here. It is interesting to note that, although the names of religious fads change, the methods and results are essentially alike. Just so with this new Prophetic movement. Initially, there is a renewed religious excitement as prophets go forth and tell the bored church members what they wanted to hear, even though they can't confirm the validity of their pronouncements through "plain old doctrine." Next come the ego boosts that ensure the church members' participation and continuing support. An appeal to the fallen human nature's desire to be one of the select is often another part of the system as well. With the Prophetic movement, it's that the "elite" are part of the greatest generation that ever lived, and that the exploits they will be doing will bring leaders of nations to the Lord. Wow! How cool is that? To be called out of a congregation and given your own personal word from God, to have hands laid on you, told you're special, and have "imparted" to you the power to do great things in the name of the Lord is heady indeed. Such an experience is comparable, in the flesh, to intoxication. No wonder people can't think straight after imbibing false teaching! Who wouldn't want to feel that he was elite enough to bring monumental change into individual lives, and even to the world? The excitement and novelty are such that people have been traveling the length and breadth of the globe, to conferences and meetings, wherever new anointed prophets are reputed to be.

According to the new prophets, we can all learn to prophesy. Techniques are now being taught in prophetic thought, dream interpretation, visualization and allegorical hermeneutics. Major prophetic impartations are being conferred on whole churches, and the decade of the restoration of the prophets has already passed!

The prophecies are almost never negative; they always portray the coming "outpouring," the coming "Great Last Days Revival," and how great the church will soon be. Ironically, the only negative pronouncements are directed toward those who would question this supposed "great anointing."

Well, one can hear just so many comforting words, and go to so many conferences, before the novelty wears off. It's like anything else in life—you can only ride the high for so long, then reality sets in. You find that the experiences that sent you into spiritual ecstasy the first few times now seem borderline hum-drum. It gets harder and harder to recapture that first sense of spiritual intoxication. For some, they just keep hopping from one conference, etc., to another, getting their latest "fix," propping up their struggling egos with fresh "words of the Lord," hoping with each new laying on of hands that the excitement, the joy, the power of those first few times will happen again.

How very sad. They have become akin to those who are "ever learning, and never able to come to the knowledge of the truth" (2 Timothy 3:7). That's not to say that everyone who is deceived and follows hard after false teaching is an unbeliever. But many likely are. An easy believism, coupled with an overarching spiritual pride, does indeed mark many who call themselves Christian yet deny the very Christ who bought them.

Again, one thing leads to another, and hence, at their final appearance before the Lord, the many deceived ones will say . . .

Didn't We Cast Out Devils?

ENTER A SPIRITUAL WARFARE movement. Ah, we don't just prophesy, nor do we merely receive prophecies. We cast out devils. And like everything else our generation approaches, we don't do it in a run-of-the-mill fashion, casting one low level demon imp out of one lowly person! We do it on a really big scale, casting demons out of whole cities! I have documented this in my first book, *Making War in the Heavenlies: A Different Look at Spiritual Warfare*. Through the teachings of C. Peter Wagner, Dick Bernal, Francis Frangipane, John Dawson and a host of others, a dualistic "spiritual warfare" doctrine has developed. By that, I mean that there is the concept that we are to battle directly with the principalities, to the point where we name them, researching the history of cities and even nations, to learn the characteristics of these "strongmen," so that we could dislodge them, and "take the city for God."

David Yonggi Cho, pastor of the world's largest Christian congregation, has taught the concept of an "open heaven," in which the atmosphere has been cleansed of all demonic entities, and there is no hindrance to the gospel. This has led to a number of symbolic actions by the church, in attempts to cleanse these heavens. These symbolic actions have run the gamut of the bizarre. A key technique is to fan out across a major city in groups, climb to the highest geographical locations, including the top of buildings, and then at a set time, collectively proclaiming a rebuke to the perceived geographical "strongman."

There was also utilized the now-defunct "March for Jesus" movement (whose founders admitted, was never about evangelism, but an attempt to "cleanse the heavenlies"), and the studying of Greek and Roman mythology, on the basis that we need to know our enemies, and that those gods are demonic spirits.

The ultimate end that this new spiritual warfare has brought us is "identificational repentance," the symbolic acknowledgement and repentance of the sins of our ancestors to the descendants of those people whom our ancestors oppressed. C. Peter Wagner wrote an article on the subject stating that this is the church's power to "change the past!"[1]

The new spiritual warfare is supposedly a whole lot more efficient than one-on-one evangelism, where you actually have to engage people with ideas, and you have to find out from them what they actually believe. Not only is this way considered profoundly boring, it takes time and it is humbling, for you could be rejected! Why mess around on that level when we can go right to the top, and "cast down" the area's head honcho, the strongman! This whole line of reasoning is ludicrous. So, are we currently so anointedthat we can actually mapping out whole nations, naming their prevailing spirits and focusing our energies against them? Where is the critical thinking here?

The old paradigm for spiritual warfare was Paul in Athens, Corinth, Ephesus, or Peter in Jerusalem: they were "opening and alleging," debating and disputing, reasoning and persuading. To the Jews they would quote the Scriptures; to the pagans they were willing to appeal to creation, conscience and even quote a few pagan poets who got it right on a given point. (Even a broken clock is right twice a day!) This is the meaning of 2 Corinthians 10:5, which speaks of "casting down imaginations, and every high thing that exalteth itself against the knowledge of God, and bringing into captivity every thought to the obedience of Christ." In short, their spiritual warfare was in the realm of the minds of men, challenging and engaging the philosophies, religions and emotional and intellectual barriers that prevented the unbelievers from being saved. Paul didn't know that all he had to do was come against "lust" in Corinth, Jezebel spirits in Jerusalem, "witchcraft" in Ephesus, and "intellectual spirits" in Athens. Paul was a Roman citizen and yet he didn't even have the humility to apologize to the Greeks or Syrians on behalf of Rome, which had virtually plundered the whole world! He didn't counsel the Romans to do that either.

No, the new model is the Argentine revival of the 1990s, which the spiritual warfare people believed had come as a result of the new spiritual warfare practices. Wagner says,

> More than any place I know, the most prominent Christian leaders in Argentina, such as Omar Cabrerro and Carlos Annacondia, Hector Giminez and others, overtly challenge and curse Satan and his demonic forces both in private prayer and in public platforms. The nation as a whole is engaged in a world class power encounter.[2]

This of course is a direct violation of the teaching of Jude 9 and 2 Peter 2:10 which warns us of willful, proud and boastful false teachers who are not afraid to despise dominions. And who are these dominions? Satan and the demonic hierarchy.

> Yet Michael the Archangel, when contending with the devil he disputed about the body of Moses, durst not bring against him a railing accusation, but said, The Lord rebuke thee, but these speak evil of those things which they know not (Jude 9).

Satan is God's problem, and God will deal with him in His own time and way.

So far, the weak view of salvation (without real conviction) has filled the churches with false converts, who need to be entertained and flattered. This has led to the Prophetic movement. But again, one can only hear so many flattering prophecies; a person has to feel like he is doing something significant. Evangelism is out of the question, since it moves too slowly, and you have to be willing to think, and possibly be rejected, and the results are often dismal. Ah, but enter spiritual warfare, whose dualistic nature with its focus on Jezebel, Saul spirits, the sins of our ancestors, and symbolic actions, and you have at your fingertips the answer to world unbelief! This movement has opened people to new mystical experiences, which will prompt them to say,

Didn't We Do Many Wonders?

WE COULDN'T STAY AT any of these points for very long, for they are part of a river, moving along, and they will take us somewhere. The mysticism of the new spiritual warfare movement prepared us for the wave of "revival" we are currently experiencing. In light of the modern churchgoer's love for extravagant manifestations of "God's presence," the question that would arise is, "Didn't we do wonders?" That's what much of this love for mystical revival is about. Unfortunately, those enamored of signs and wonders consider them self-validating. In today's thinking, miracles show that God is at work in a particular congregation. And, because God is at work there, then there are signs and wonders. It is circular reasoning at its finest

Of course we have had to change our thinking in order to be able to receive this. Almost twenty years ago, John Wimber was calling for a paradigm shift in the church. A paradigm shift means a change in worldview, or a change in the whole way a person perceives reality! John Goodwin was a Vineyard pastor almost from its inception, and traveled extensively with Wimber for years. In his article entitled "Testing the Fruit of the Vineyard" he explains the paradigm shift that Wimber called for:

> According to Wimber, in order for us to fully appreciate what God is doing in the world, we must experience what he calls a "paradigm shift" from a Western way of thinking, to an Eastern way of looking at things . . . This paradigm shift is explained by Wimber in his seminar on "Signs And Wonders and Church Growth" in what he calls a "logic syllogism." Presuming that people in the far east have an "eastern" or experiential mind set, he describes an exchange of logic with an imaginary far easterner with the following result: You tell someone from the far or middle east that cotton only grows in warm, semi-arid climates. England is cold and wet. [Ask them] Does cotton grow in England? The answer you'll get is, "I don't know, I haven't been to England."[3]

The shift is from a logical and rational approach to life to a purely experiential approach. This did more to open people up to the mysticism in the now-fizzled "Toronto Blessing" and its offshoot, the Brownsville Revival, than anything else. In this new paradigm, the way God changes a life is redefined. Under the old paradigm of orthodox Christianity, with its "the truth shall make you free" and "The Son of God is come, and hath given us an understanding" speaks of propositional truth. God has spoken unto us in His Son, He sent His Word, His Logos, and healed us. But the New Paradigm rejects all of that as necessary for a changed life. These days people are getting zapped!

> I went down to Pensacola, and I didn't even believe in this stuff, but as soon as I came through the door, my legs started shaking, my arms started trembling, I started twitching and ever since then, I have been consumed with a burning desire to be "intimate with Jesus!"

Truth, in a logo-centric, propositional form, counts for nothing in the New Paradigm. Adherence to the Word is considered legalism, and is for those churches that are dead, dry and "mainlining on prunes" as Rodney Howard Browne, "God's Bartender" liked to say. In the New Paradigm, it is no longer truth that changes lives, but is sheer experience. The intimation is, "Turn off your mind, don't pray, don't analyze. You wouldn't analyze a kiss from your lover would you?" This is how they put it in places like Toronto.

"Lord! Didn't we do many wonderful works?" If the reports of adherents are to be believed, then Toronto and Pensacola were so wonderful they exceeded the revival in the Book of Acts! Peter and Paul never got whole congregations so drunk they couldn't stand up, but Arnott and Kilpatrick have! You talk about signs! When did John, James or Peter ever prophesy like a roaring lion, or fly around like an eagle?

Alas, you can't stay there for long. Sooner or later, the party has to be over, the drunkenness has to wear off, and the shepherds have to slumber, so that they can be like sleeping dogs, unable to bark a warning. What next? Then they will say . . .

"My Lord Delayeth His Coming"

AND FOR THIS ONE, we have to turn to the Book of Matthew 24:48-51. When the church begins to accrue the popularity and measure of worldly success and power that it has, the Coming of Jesus Christ as an imminent reality loses its appeal. After all, what about the Great Last Days Revival? If Jesus came back tonight, what about all the prophecies that say we are going to come into a time where the average believer will be like Elijah, and our prophets and apostles will have names that nations will "tremble at the sound of?" Then, in the heart, comes the thought that "My lord delayeth his coming."

Many of us have heard the exhortations that "Christ isn't coming for us until He comes within us! We have to come into the glory, before the actual coming of Christ, so these 'words' will come to pass! Don't talk to me about some 'helicopter escape,' with your old rapture theory! I don't want to escape! We are the cutting-edge, glorious, advancing church!" And so goes the man-exalting seduction, contrary to Jesus' solemn exhortation in Luke 21:36,

> Watch ye therefore, and pray always, that ye may be accounted worthy to escape all these things that shall come to pass and to stand before the Son of Man.

With the loss of an imminent hope, there is a casting about for a new hope and meaning, which expresses itself in two distinct ways. One way your hope is in mysticism, an attempt at oneness with God, through sensual spirituality, that culminates in the abomination of ". . . to eat and drink with the drunken," which we have already noted.

The other way is the hope in a highly hierarchical church, with its premise of "(he) shall begin to smite his fellowservants." I look for the emergence of a new strain of the hyper-shepherding movement, in a man-centered attempt to bring structure to the chaos that Toronto and Pensacola have wrought. There are signs of such abuse right now, for the newly exalted prophets and apostles are assuming unique authority. There are now those who assume to be the "elder" or "apostle" of a given city. These positions have actually been conferred on them by the false traveling prophets.

Years ago, I was at a meeting of pastors in my city who had been invited to hear Rick Joyner. The pastor who had invited them actually told the assembled pastors to be sure not to miss the evening meeting, for they (he and Joyner) had been instructed to call the pastors forward, in order to "set them into the body of Christ." The pastor of a large church in the Quad Cities had been radicalized by the new prophets, and was given to an extremely aggressive tone, berating the flock, and telling them that if they don't like the "new thing" to "get out of my face, someone else wants your seat!" This behavior was actually applauded by that part of the congregation that bought into this madness.

Bill McCartney of Promise Keepers, when announcing to a stadium of men an upcoming pastors' conference, told them that if their pastor didn't want to support this, he needs to be able to tell them why not. There is a new strong spirit of arrogance. Partly this is because, I think, many pastors are feeling new importance by all of the self-aggrandizing ministry they are bringing into their churches. But I also think that in the back of their minds, many of them are condemned because they have brought their churches into this mystical river, knowing it wasn't right, but afraid that they would lose out on all of the excitement, success, and popularity. Therefore in their spiritual hangovers, in between meetings and religious fads, they beat their fellow servants. God help them.

Is there any other way? Do we have to be carried down the river, to this end? I am sure that no one dreamed in the beginning that they would be at the point of screaming at their churches, to "Get out of my face! Others want your seat!" What pastor would drive away those who would, in many cases, be some of the best people? People who have given their lives, time, money, and raised their children in the very church whose pastor now berates them for not "jumping into the River?" What kind of revival is this?

If there is another way to go, it would have to begin with humility. If I could speak face-to-face with false revival adherents, I'd say to them, "Let's face it— you have been bewitched. Go back to the Word of God. Get away from the seducing notion that we are so special, that we are going to be great, and just be willing to become a redeemed human being again, washed in the blood of the Lamb, and under the Word of God. It may well be that there is still time to come back, to simple, beautiful, Orthodox Christianity. All we really have is Jesus and His promises, but that is all we have ever needed. I am no prophet, but I do offer you a proven Word from the Lord,

> In that day shalt thou not be ashamed for all thy doings, wherein thou hast transgressed against me: for then I will take away out of the midst of thee them that rejoice in thy pride, and thou shalt no more be haughty because of my holy mountain.

> I will also leave in the midst of thee an afflicted and poor people, and they shall trust in the name of the LORD. The remnant of Israel shall not do iniquity, nor speak lies; neither shall a deceitful tongue be found in their mouth; for they shall feed and lie down, and none shall make them afraid.

> Sing, O daughter of Zion; shout, O Israel; be glad and rejoice with all the heart, O daughter of Jerusalem.

> The LORD hath taken away thy judgments, he hath cast out thine enemy: the king of Israel, even the LORD, is in the midst of thee . . . (Zephaniah 3:11-15).

Grace and peace be with you."

Appendix 1

Zowie, Zoe! Here's My Money!

This article provided by
Al Dager from Media Spotlight Volume 21, No 1.

BEING ON THE MAILING list for many organizations, not all of whom we agree with, we find some interesting things in the mail. One "ministry," Zoe, headed by "Bishop" and "prophet" Bernard Jordan, graced us with its "Countdown to Prophetic Congress" daily calendar. As one tears off one day to reveal the next, one encounters "prophetic" statements and instructions for life, some of which we felt led to share with our readers. The first quoted are pure science of mind:

> January 1, 1998: You are the sum of your thoughts.

> January 2, 1998: Your present life is a reflection of yesterday's thoughts.

> December 22, 1998: The Bible teaches you to practice auto-suggestion and autohypnosis.

> December 24, 1998: The woman with the issue of blood hypnotized herself.

> December 26/27 1998: Her wholeness came because she gave life to a thought.

The word/faith element of Jordan's teachings is also evident:

January 23, 1998: The law works whether you are righteous or unrighteous.
[This implies immutable spiritual laws into which anyone can tap.]

January 27, 1998: Stop looking for power outside of yourself.
[Thanks, but I'll look to the Father for His power. Yes, the Holy Spirit indwells you if you are born again by His Spirit, but He is not "yourself."]

January 30, 1998: Your thoughts can establish whatever form you desire.
[In other words, you can create reality using your mind.]

February 20, 1998: The universe will assure that you get just what you deserve.
[This is Hindu karma. If everyone got just what they deserved, no one would be saved. I thank God that I won't get what I deserve!]

March 3, 1998: Your mind has unlimited power.
[That's not true, thank God! Without God the imagination of man is only evil continually (Genesis 6:5).]

March 6, 1998: Your ability to think reflects the Presence of God.
[With a capital "P" the Presence of God means the person of God. But Hitler had the ability to think. So does Satan. Think about it.]

March 7/8, 1998: Your mind is operating in its full ability to think when you become aware of your Christhood.

[There is only one Christ-Jesus. I have no Christhood, and neither does Bernard Jordan. This is New Age philosophy.]

March 10, 1998: Your mind possesses the power to move things without the assistance of your physical hands.
[Okay, Jordan, let's see you move something without using your hands. Occultists are the only ones who claim this power, and the source is either Satan or his demons.]

March 12, 1998: Your mind can start res.(?)

March 16, 1998:The mind is capable of bending spoons.
[What are we to seek—a carnival act? What good comes from bending spoons?]

April 14, 1998: The fruit of conception will reflect the state of consciousness you were in.
[In other words (combined with other sayings preceding this one), your child will reflect the sum of your thoughts at the time he is conceived.]

April 28, 1998: The devil cannot manifest until you, the I am, connect your I am to that which is other than God.
[Jesus is the "I am," not man.]

Encouraging self-love and speaking of how we allegedly create our own enemies as reflections of ourselves, Jordan leads into this one:

May 23/24, 1998: An enemy can only manifest as an expression of your own self-hatred.
[Didn't Jesus have enemies? Was he filled with self-hatred? He told us that the world would hate us if we followed after Him.

Jordan's concept of hell is also telling:

July 9, 1998: Your decisions will make your own heaven or hell.

July 10, 1998: Heaven is a state of satisfaction, whereas hell is a perpetual state of confusion.

July 18/19, 1998: Hell is not outside of God, but hell is in God.

August 8/9, 1998: God and the devil are one.
[This blasphemy reveals Jordan's god as the Force, possessing both a light and a dark side.]

Of course, don't think that you can receive everything free from this "prophet." Every month contains repeated instructions on certain days that prompt the person to send money.

For example, each month has a "Special Offer":

Are you concerned about your family's destiny? Sow a $365.00 seed, and hear what God is saying about your family over the next year!

One day each month offers the following opportunity:

Send in your Miracle Seed of $98.00, your date of birth and your most pressing question! I will prophesy your answer on cassette tape.

How much are you willing to bet that the cassette tapes contain generalizations to all possible questions depending upon the date of one's birth (and that multiple days of birth contain the same messages)? Maybe so, maybe not; I wasn't going to spend the money to find out how this astrological ploy manifests itself.

In addition to these monthly appeals for money, Jordan offers a series of audio tapes on meditation for $500, a number of workbooks for $50 per volume, and encouragement to register for the upcoming "Prophetic Congress" to be held August 24-27, 1999.

To charge money for a "prophetic word" from God is as evil as charging money for indulgences of God's grace, as has been the practice of Roman Catholicism. It was a major issue of the Reformation.

It comes as no surprise, therefore, that "Bishop" Jordan regales himself in a mitre hat, papal robes and a shepherd's staff, as does the pope of Rome. The same spirit works in both.

Appendix 2

The Source of the River: Are Toronto and Pensacola Equal?

THE CURRENT REVIVAL MOVEMENT which has swept the Charismatic and Pentecostal and even the Evangelical world, is often likened unto a river, even the River of God! The Psalmist tells us that truly, "There is a river, the streams whereof shall make glad the city of God," and all who truly love our Lord Jesus long for that river of living water. This is why we must seriously consider the claims of the proponents of the revival which broke out at the Brownsville Assembly of God, in Pensacola, Florida (BAOG) on Father's Day of 1995. It would be presumptuous of us to simply dismiss the accounts of lives changed, dramatic encounters with God, and even decreases in the crime rates of certain cities, as well as a host of other "signs and wonders." After all, many of us have been crying out for revival for many years, and a revival is needed to shake out the complacency that has plagued the church for too long. However, it would be equally presumptuous to "jump in with both feet," merely on the basis of the excitement that seems to be rejuvenating bored Christians and churches. We are commanded to judge all things, in the light of the Scriptures. It would do us well to ponder the actual source of the "River," for in things spiritual, origin determines validity. Not only by their fruits, but by their roots shall we know them, for "A good tree cannot bring forth evil fruit, neither can a corrupt tree bring forth good fruit" (Matthew 7:18).

Where does this River come from? And where will it be taking those many thousands of believers, and even churches, who have jumped into it? What streams flow into it, and with what larger current does it converge? There are divided views as to the meaning of this revival. Some see this as a sovereign move of God, and in some cases, the long awaited and prophesied, "Great Last Days Revival." But there are others who imply, and in some cases come right out and say, that this is part of the "delusion" of Second Thessalonians 2. Then there are those who take a third track—they don't care where the river comes from, and to them all that matters are the apparent "results" that are occurring in many lives and churches. They live by the code of "It works, so don't knock it." In other words, the end justifies the means.

This article seeks to answer these questions, and in particular the charge that the "River" is the direct outflow of what is known in apologetic circles as the Latter Rain/Manifested Sons of God heresy. My only qualifications are that I am a Christian believer, and a pastor, who has written two books that seek to speak to similar and related phenomenon. My first book, *Making War in the Heavenlies, A Different Look at Spiritual Warfare*, written in 1994, was written to give my reasons for rejecting the spiritual warfare movement of the mid 1980s. Although I do believe that we are engaged in spiritual warfare, practices such as spiritual mapping, identifying the "strongman" over a given geographical location, challenging demon powers by name and rank, praise marches, driving stakes to claim cities for God, and a host of other practices that became intensely popular in the late 1980s and early 1990s, have more to do with magic and mysticism than they do with New Testament spirituality. When did Peter or Paul ever research the history of a city that they sought to evangelize, so that they could fight the "ruling spirits?" When did they ever challenge, curse or rebuke Zeus, Apollos, or any of the rest of the Pantheon? I assure you that they had ample opportunity!

My second book, *Weighed and Found Wanting*, dealt with the

revival of outright mysticism, called the Toronto Blessing (TB), or the laughing revival. In my research, I found that the TB has descended from a long line of mysticism and erroneous teaching that goes back at least forty years. Starting with the Vineyard Movement itself, and moving back to the teaching of the late John Wimber, and further to the Kansas City Prophets, and their personal prophecies, and prophetic schools, then to a man who dubs himself, "God's Bartender," Rodney Howard Browne, (heavily influenced by the Word of Faith error). The influences that have led to the TB were varied, ranging from C. P. Wagner's church growth movement, and spiritual warfare teachings, all the way over to Paul Cain, the protégé` of William Branham, out of whose ministry came the Latter Rain/Manifested Sons of God heresy, long renounced by the Assemblies of God.

This is what brings us to our current subject, and the question posed: Is Pensacola more of the same? Is this just another laughing revival, or Latter Rain? First I will give a brief account of the Pensacola Revival, especially a look at how it began, and the early influences. Then, I'll offer a brief overview of MSOG teaching, which has infiltrated much of contemporary evangelical ministry, and captivated much of the Christian media.

The Pensacola Revival is the direct outcome of the Toronto Blessing, as the events that lead up to Fathers Day, 1995, show (the official beginning of the Pensacola revival). Previously, Steve Hill and the leadership of the Brownsville Assembly of God had gone up to Toronto to receive the "anointing" there. As the following article, (publication unknown) demonstrates, changes had already begun in the church, as a result of Brenda Kilpatrick's visit to Toronto.

> Strange, unusual and wonderful things started happening after Brenda Kilpatrick came back from the Vineyard church in Toronto, Canada . . . signs of early revival started manifesting in the spring services . . . What had been seen in Toronto started happening

> among the people of Brownsville . . . Brenda explained
> how she had a drastic change in her prayer life. "I could
> never be the same again after I returned from Toronto."

She then proceeds to tell one of these "wonderful things,"
such as being frozen in one position for over two hours!

From several other inside accounts, it seems plain that this
revival did not take anyone by surprise, there was a great deal of
anticipation, and that something along the lines of the Toronto
Blessing was going to happen at the Brownsville Assembly of God
Church in Pensacola. The reason this needs to be emphasized
is that one is often given the impression that "Suddenly, like a
rushing mighty wind," the Spirit blew in on an unsuspecting
Pentecostal church, actually hitting the pastor in the back of the
legs and knocking him over, and turning a one-day preaching
engagement into a three year series of continuous meetings, to
everyone's complete surprise! On the contrary, it is obvious that
something was expected of the Steve Hill meetings. From the
same article we learn that

> The time had come for God to allow his move at the
> Pensacola church, and Brenda explained how it came
> about. "We had a friend named Steve Hill . . . he called
> us about his impartation that he had received from
> England. He was just on fire with a new anointing of
> what God had given him. We were so excited and said,
> 'maybe this will bring revival when Steve comes . . .'"

Like Brenda Kilpatrick, the pastor's wife, Steve Hill had also
been to Toronto to receive an anointing, having been prayed for
by Carol Arnott. But it was not until he received an anointing in
an upscale Anglican church in England, Holy Trinity Brompton,
that the Pensacola revival was imparted to Hill. Holy Trinity
Brompton (HTB) church is the fountainhead for what you
are seeing at Brownsville, for it was there that Hill received his

anointing. Hill had first read about HTB in an article in *Time* magazine (of all places) entitled "Laughing for the Lord."

> Though pathetically tiny flocks of Londoners attend many Anglican services, Holy Trinity Brompton has a standing room only turnout of 1500 . . . After the usual scripture readings, prayers and singing, the chairs are cleared away. Curate Nicky Gumbel prays that the Holy Spirit will come upon the congregation. Soon a young woman begins laughing. Others gradually join her with hearty belly laughs. A young worshiper falls to the floor, hands twitching . . . within half an hour there are bodies everywhere as supplicants sob, roar like lions, and strangest of all, laugh uncontrollably . . . this frenzied display has become known as the laughing revival, or Toronto blessing . . . After first appearing at Holy Trinity Brompton only last May, laughing revivals have been reported in Anglican parishes from Manchester to York to Brighton.[1]

The very service that launched the Pensacola revival was basically Hill's recounting of how he received the impartation, at HTB. Hill was stopping over in London, and was to stay with friends. Like many thousands of godly and dedicated ministers of the gospel, he was battle-weary, tired and even spiritually hungry. Reading the *Time* article sparked something in him. He asked his British hosts, "Where is the Holy Ghost moving in England?" His hosts happened to be members of HTB, and they loaded him down with literature concerning the revival that HTB was experiencing as a result of Toronto. As Hill began to read, "testimony after testimony" of the lives changed and faith renewed, his hunger only increased. But he needed Scripture, so he opened his Bible to the Book of Acts and read, "Have you received the Holy Ghost since you believed?" This seemed to be a confirmation, but he needed more, so he turned to another

Scripture and found where it was written that Aquila and Priscilla were showing Apollos the more excellent way, which Hill interpreted as them saying, "There's more!" That was enough for him, so he made an appointment with Sandy Millar, the pastor of HTB. Arriving at the church in the middle of a prayer meeting, Hill was amazed at the sight of it. He recounts:

> I stepped over bodies to get to the pastor. When Sandy touched me I fell to the ground. (I don't ever do that) . . . I was like a kid at TOYS'R'US . . . then I got up and ran to a couple and said "Pray for me, man, this is good!" they touched me and WHAM! I went back down. Some of you God is going to hit in a powerful way. If you are hungry, get prayed for a dozen times.[2]

In England and in much of the English-speaking world, HTB is synonymous with Toronto Blessing. Even the secular press recognized it, as you saw in *Time* magazine. The very name "Toronto Blessing" was coined by a staffer at HTB. There has been much press coverage of the HTB/Toronto Blessing for example, in an article excerpt from a secular British publication entitled, "Congregation Rolling in the Aisle" by Nicholas Monson. He writes:

> It was my second visit to HTB and I was nervous . . . it was my friend Claire who reawakened my interest. She told me how the week before, the Holy Spirit had entered people in the church. She explained that this was because a church in Toronto had started to have visitations, and the enterprising clergy of HTB had flown over and literally seemed to have brought some of the Holy Ghost back with them.[3]

And this from the *Daily Mail*, an article entitled, "This Man Has Been Given the Toronto Blessing: What in God's Name is Going On?" by Geoffrey Levy.

[HTB] is a place of worship that has attracted large congregations . . . with verbal offerings by the Curate Nicky Gumbel such as "Jesus blows your mind." It must be said that soon after word of the Toronto Blessing reached them, that does appear to be what Jesus did.

The Christian press also, confirms this connection. *Alpha* magazine, a British evangelical publication, in an article on the TB entitled "Rumours of Revival" began with a description of a May, 1994 service at HTB. *Charisma* magazine, in a February, 1995 article entitled "A Wave of the Spirit" by Clive Price states of Vicar Sandy Millar that, "It wasn't until Millar went to Toronto that he experienced God afresh."

In an interview in *The Destiny Image Digest*, Steve Hill, when asked to compare the Toronto and Pensacola revivals, replied,

Well I love John and Carol Arnott and I love Sandy Millar. I've been to both places and I believe they are both undergoing sovereign moves of God. I received a wonderful refreshing in Holy Trinity and I have been up to Toronto, where I had Carol Arnott pray for me. But we are dealing with different areas of the world . . . John and Carol Arnott came down here with members of their staff to visit us. When he said, "Steve we want to see more of the evangelistic thrust," I shared with him, "God is using you brother, to touch the world right now. I don't think anybody needs to be duplicating anybody else, and I don't think that's the problem." We've received a lot from the Toronto church on how to pray with people and care for folks. We model a lot of what is going on here from them.

As you can tell, there is a tendency to acknowledge Toronto, yet at the same time imply that there is a difference between the two revivals. But as I have demonstrated, Pensacola owes much to the Toronto Blessing. Not only did the leadership there make their own pilgrimages to the Airport Vineyard, the primary impartation that is the basis for the "River" came from HTB church, an Anglican church which was radicalized by the Toronto Blessing and became a major figure in its propagation.

Appendix 3

The Crazy World
of Gerald Coates

By Neil Richardson

Material taken from two articles in *Vanguard Magazine*
PO Box LB1475, Egham W1A 9LB UK

IN THE 1970S THE so called "house church" movement began in England. Most of these churches operate under the banner of "Restorationism," and show a commitment to restore the pattern of ministry of the NT churches, especially with regard to the ministries of Ephesians 4:11, including apostleship. Gerald Coates became a leader in the "R2" branch of this movement: that is, the part that believes in fully engaging with popular culture as a means of evangelism, and also so that it may be enjoyed for its own sake. [see Andrew Walker's book, *Restoring the Kingdom*]

Gerald Coates, a former postman, now lives in a substantial country mansion at Cobham, Surrey. He and a number of other prominent leaders, such as John and Christine Noble and the eminent medical expert, Patrick Dixon, work together under the umbrella title of "Pioneer" churches.

There is an emphasis in these churches on community action and social justice; prominent roles for women in leadership; demonstration of the supernatural gifts, especially tongues and the giving of prophecies, words of knowledge or "pictures"; Vineyard-style rock-pop worship, with the worship leader being a sustained and central focal point; the "slain in the spirit," "carpet time," "holy laughter" and other Toronto-style experiences.

The theology stresses the Holy Spirit; endtimes eschatology (namely, post-millennial Kingdom Now dogma, where the Church is expected to rise up and Christianise the world before the return of Christ); Revivalism; signs and wonders in gospel preaching (power evangelism); and—in the view of many—seriously underplays the authority of Scripture and the centrality of the message of Christ and Him Crucified.

Coates set up, with Roger Forster of Ichthus, Lynn Green of YWAM and the songwriter Graham Kendrick, March for Jesus which has now become a global phenomenon each summer. The thinking behind this is in line with another project of theirs, Operation A-Z. In both ventures, the view is that by moving geographically over the earth, somehow spiritual principalities and powers that are believed to be residing in or over these areas are vanquished. This is popularly known as "claiming the ground," and is refuted superbly in a book by Chuck Lowe, published by OMF. The idea finds its most vocal manifestation in C. Peter Wagner of the Church Growth-dominated Fuller Theological Seminary in the US.

Coates has latterly furthered strengthened links with the US "Prophetic Movement." He has been staging for over a year now Big Top, US-style Revival meetings in Westminster, which he sees as a key location or "spiritual stronghold" in England (as it is the seat of secular government). His fascination for this area led him to make a false prophecy concerning massive revival at Westminster Chapel, led by the Kentucky-born minister RT Kendall. This revival never took place, though Westminster Chapel under Kendall's leadership have gone further into the apostasy by linking up with Rodney Howard-Browne (originator of the Toronto Experience), Paul Cain (former Kansas City Prophet) and HTB, the church that first launched the Toronto and Pensacola experiences in England, and is responsible for the ecumenical and theologically defective

Alpha Course, now almost universally acclaimed in the UK and worldwide as the sine qua non of evangelistic tools. At Coates' Revival meetings, several American personalities have peddled their wares, most notably Wayne Drain, Dale Gentry and Clark Pinnock, who has caused waves with his theology of God, in which he states that God neither has knowledge nor power over the future and—staggeringly—might even lose the cosmic battle against Satan were it not for our help. Coates has most recently shifted to the Royal Albert Hall, and is charging folks money to go and hear his stories of revival from around the world (by which he means the successful hyping of the flock into psychosomatic signs and wonders and group hysteria; this is perhaps most evident in South America under the leadership of such men as Claudio Freidzon).

Coates is also the author of several maverick and often self-regarding books, such as *The Intelligent Fire* (his autobiography—he is not yet 50), *The Vision*, *Kingdom Now* and *Non-religious Christianity*. From a brethren background, his criticisms of "mainstream" or "institutional" Christianity are not infrequent, and often not lacking in perception or grounds.

With acknowledgements to *Charismatics and the Next Millennium* by Nigel Scotland Hodder & Stoughton 1995.

Introduction

"Many Christians prefer to be spoilt by praise than saved by criticism," observes Gerald Coates in *The Vision*. This article fully intends to test Mr Coates' adherence to this principle! In an attempt to forestall the classic objection—"Yes, but have you read this by him . . ."—every attempt has been made to build up as broad and thorough a picture of Gerald and his teachings as possible.

The sources used are therefore:

- *Gerald Quotes*, (Gerald Coates, 1984, Kingsway; abbv: GQ)

- *An Intelligent Fire*, (Gerald Coates, 1991, Kingsway; abbv: IF)
- *Kingdom Now*, (Gerald Coates, 1993, Kingsway; abbv: KN)
- "Toronto and Scripture," (Gerald Coates, 1994, article in *Renewal*, reprinted in *The Impact of Toronto* edited by Wallace Boulton)
- *The Vision, an antidote to post-charismatic depression*, (Gerald Coates, 1995, Kingsway; abbv: Vis)
- *Non religious Christianity*, (Gerald Coates, 1995, Word Books, abbv: NC)
- *A Breath of Fresh Air*, (Mike Fearon, 1994, Eagle)
- *Charismatics and the Next Millennium*, (Nigel Scotland, 1995, Hodder & Stoughton; abbv: 'Sc')
- *Signs of Revival*, (Patrick Dixon, 1994, Kingsway)
- The Pioneer website on the Internet (http://ds.dial. pipex.com/pioneerpeople/).
- *Evangelicals Now*, July 1996 (Bulldog column) and February 1997 ('False prophecy today?')
- "Rumours of Revival" video (presented by Coates, 1995, Word videos)
- "Sowing the Seeds of Revival" videos (May/June 1997, with Coates and Dale Gentry).
- A brief talk with Mr Coates at a Sowing the Seeds of Revival meeting, (25 June 1997)
- Discussion on Radio 4's Sunday the morning after the Wembley Stadium gig, "The Champion of the World," (28 June 1997)

Of this material, Scotland's *Charismatics and the Next Millennium* is highly recommended as an encyclopedia of the movement. Rumours of Revival is a inadvertently self-damning promotion of the Toronto Experience. *An Intelligent Fire* (Coates' autobiography) is probably the most astonishingly egotistical and self-regarding book I have ever read.

Gerald the Fabulist

GERALD HAS NO FIXED doctrine of revelation or of Scripture, and thence no clear understanding of the character of God. We must examine Gerald's "pick and mix' or "make it up as you go along" approach to theology. Gerald, like so many others, utterly reveres that "fat man just trying to get to heaven" (in his own words) the late John Wimber. This explains why Gerald goes firmly along with Wimber's "we are cataloguing all of our experiences so we can develop a theology." I suggest that the epidemic awe in which John Wimber is held by people like Gerald is not because of his sound, passionate Gospel preaching. It is not because of his soul-winning exposition of the Word of God. It is not because he has decided to glory in the cross of Christ (which initially was not mentioned in Power Evangelism!). It is because he gets "results." Jeremiah's lack of converts and Job's devastating losses would relegate both of them to the very bottom of the prophetic heap today. No, Wimber lives by faith, and look how big and successful Vineyard is. They have all the good music, and all the exotic experiences.

Gerald is also totally obsessed with numbers. What impresses him about Billy Graham is the 27,000 a night attendance (Earls Court, 1966). His unadvisedly-named "Festival of Light" (is that a Hindu thing?) was fantastic because of the "30,000 who swelled Trafalgar Square [and] another group of several thousand" (IF, 83). Come Together ("a prophetic statement about the unity of the body of Christ" apparently) was held in Westminster Central Hall "crammed with over 2,500 people." We must commend Gerald for his incomparable ability to organise large groups of excitable people together, but numbers are very different from true spiritual fruit. And the hubris generated is unbearable:

> If the house church movement was the most significant movement in the church in the seventies, the Nationwide Festival of Light and Come Together were the two major projects of the decade. (IF, 93).

Strange that the two major projects of the decade were both run by Gerald Coates, and that he doesn't inch from telling us so in his autobiography. (It takes a lot of chutzpah to find your self a worthy subject of a book in any case, but as Gerald cites Anatole France, "A writer is rarely so well inspired as when he talks about himself." Gerald really should read the Bible: "Let another man praise thee, and not thine own mouth; a stranger, and not thine own lips" (Proverbs 27:2).

Gerald's ambition for big crowds following him about is seemingly insatiable. [Gerald doesn't seem to mind citing this comparison of him with a certain German chancellor . . . "Mr Gerald Coates, who kept the continuity between the different parts of the rally, often encouraged the audience to give its festival salute, in the form of a raised arm and hand, rather reminiscent of the salute performed at a different sort of rally just over thirty years age."] He's now succeeded in filling Wembley Stadium, the largest venue in the UK ("The Champion of the World," 28 June 1997). Where next?! But I have to confess, isn't there some confusion as to who the champion is? The Lord Jesus for His sacrificial death and triumphant resurrection, or Gerald for filling a stadium of happy clappers?

The problem with a results-and-numbers-based theology is twofold. First, "if I still pleased men, I would not be a servant of Christ" (Galatians 1:10) and "woe to you when all men speak well of you, for so did their fathers to the false prophets" (Luke 6:26). Second, when the numbers aren't there, what's going to become of us? Our security is not in the Lord, but in "how many we can influence." Gerald will increasingly find that in order to fill stadia, he will have to "heap up for them teachers . . . and they will turn their ears away from the truth, and be turned aside to fables" (2 Timothy 4:3-4). Gerald is proud to be a storyteller, a fabulist, if it gets bums on chairs: "I'm a prophet, not a Bible teacher."

But Just What Kind of Prophet is Gerald?

PROPHECY I:

"Dr Kendall—in eighteen months from this month (April 1995) your church, Westminster Chapel, will be unrecognisable, completely and totally unrecognisable . . . the Holy Spirit will increase in power [How can the Holy Spirit of God increase in power? Only other spirits can have their influence enlarged or diminished by God's sovereign permission. NR.] In 18 months (October 1996) the Spirit of God—not just upon Westminster Chapel, but upon Westminster itself, upon the high of the land, upon many who live in that area, is going to come on that place and many of your prayers—taxi drivers would get out of their taxis because the Spirit of God is so strong in that place—you're going to see them fullfilled. And it will come from the most unlikely sources, it will not come through the people you would like it to be through, it'll come through the most unlikely sources. And if you keep your heart and your eyes open the Spirit of God is going to surprise us all." (Given at Spring Harvest, April 20 1995; circulated by Kendall at Westminster Chapel in December 1995).

OUTCOME I:

"What has come of the prophecy [which] states . . . in short, that the area and the church will have been transformed by revival? [What has happened] appears to be the complete reverse of what was promised. Far from experiencing joyous revival it is report-ed that over 100 people have left Westminster Chapel since Dr Kendall's well-publicised attempt to bring the Toronto Blessing on the church. There are the dwindling numbers in the church, the continuing lack of impact on the local community and the complete absence of a godly direction taken by many among the Parliamentary "high of the land." Sadly, in anyone's book, this is tantamount to the failure of the prediction. If the prophecy did not come from God, then are we not constrained by God's Word to declare that they are the vain imaginings of a false prophet?"

(Alan Howe, "False prophecy today?" *Evangelicals Now*, February 1997—essential reading).

The writer of this article can verify this—I was one of the 100+ who left West Chap (ask to leave RT Kendall's office as the preacher raged at my daring to question the Biblical soundness of Toronto). West Chap is a shell of its former glory, and the preaching of the Word is mingled with abortive attempts to stir up the "double anointing" that RT desperately craves as, sadly, his ministry flags.

HERE'S WHAT THE BIBLE says:

1. If you prophesy something that doesn't happen, under Mosaic law, you are put to death.

> But the prophet, which shall presume to speak a word in my name, which I have not commanded him to speak, or that shall speak in the name of other gods, even that prophet shall die. And if thou say in thine heart, How shall we know the word which the LORD hath not spoken? When a prophet speaketh in the name of the LORD. if the thing follow not, nor come to pass, that is the thing which the LORD hath not spoken, but the prophet hath spoken it presumptuously: thou shalt not be afraid of him (Deuteronomy 18:20-22).

How does Gerald get round this? He has made a false prophecy, declared something in God's name which didn't happen and brought "the reproach of the heathen our enemies" (Nehemiah 5:9). Under Moses, he would already be dead. Is he sorry? Not a bit of it! He told me that West Chap was unrecognisable! Well in one sense he is right, if you want to destroy the significance of words forever. It's a bit like some builders coming round to do up your house and promising to leave it "unrecognisable." You didn't place quite the same emphasis on the word when they scarper leaving it a complete bombsite which is spiritually what Westminster Chapel is. Why can't Gerald face up to the fact that he's made a serious error (a resigning offence) and repent with humility? Because his ego and the credibility of his own word stand higher in his estimation that the warnings of Scripture and the plain facts of the matter.

2. Don't listen to prophets God hasn't sent, who fabricate fine prospects about the future with their imaginations.

> Do not listen to the words of the prophets who prophesy to you. They make you worthless; they speak a vision of their own heart, not from the mouth of the Lord. They continually say to those who despise me, "The Lord has said, 'You shall have peace'"; and to everyone who walks according to the imagination of his own heart, "No evil shall come upon you" . . . I have not sent these prophets, yet they ran. I have not spoken to them, yet they prophesied—how long will this be in the heart of the prophets who prophesy lies? Indeed they are prophets of the deceit of their own heart, who try to make my people forget my name by their dreams . . . Behold I am against prophets who use their tongues and say, "He says." . . . (Jeremiah 23).

PROPHECY II:

"In 1991 Mr Coates visited New Zealand where he informed local church leaders that God had spoken strongly to him about an earthquake that would devastate Lake Taupo. The leaders were told this would take place in April of that year. Local Elim leaders believed this prophecy and instigated a national media campaign to warn their nation. 44 Elim churches began taking survival courses. April came and went and nothing happened [Nigel Scotland confirms this: "Gerald . . . prophesied that a volcano would erupt in NZ by a particular date. It Didn't Happen (Sc, 151)]. The secular press had a field day laughing at the church and particularly evangelicalism."

(Ibid., *Evangelicals Now*)

OUTCOME II:

The earthquake didn't happen. IT DID NOT HAPPEN. What did Gerald tell me? "Because by the faith and the prayers of the leaders the earthquake was diverted"—without blinking twice! Why did they take survival courses then? Did Gerald mention anything about this in his prophecy? No.

Stunningly, Gerald decides to edit out of the Bible the bit about things not happening as being a mark of a false prophet: "No, the judgment of death on the prophet is not only given for words that do not come to pass, for there are several interpretations of what could have happened or might yet happen. A false prophet is one who leads God's people into open rebellion and idolatry. Rebellion against God and his word . . . I would suggest that almost all prophecy is conditional if not all" (*Kingdom Now*, 129-130). This appalling doctrine of convenience is akin to the prosperity gospel "if you're not healed, it's because you lack faith, not because I lack integrity or power." As Alan Howe correctly points out:

> Taken to its logical conclusion, this argument makes all prophecies completely untestable. (Ibid.)

And that's just the way Gerald wants it, especially seeing as he sets so much store by the bogus, discredited Kansas City Prophets—notably Paul Cain who "gave a prophecy which later caused great confusion and a fair amount of disillusionment among many thousands of Christians in Britain. He declared that revival would break out in London in October 1990" (Sc, 151). Of course, Cain and Wimber (who supported the prophecy until it proved itself utterly untrue) wheedled their way out of it by saying that Wimber "had misunderstood Paul Cain who prophesied 'tokens of revival' as implying something of much greater proportions" (Ibid.). The sheer nerve of Coates, Wimber and Cain takes one's breath away. They make up in audacity what they lack in veracity! They may be liars, but they're brilliant at following through the bluff.

PROPHECY III:

"There is no doubt that we are seeing the early stages of 'a world revival.'" (Patrick Dixon, Coates' whitecoat henchman—great on medical ethics, terrible about the operation of the Holy Spirit [He believes that Altered States of Consciousness . . . are the basis of dynamic, personal, relevant, living faith" (*Signs of Revival*, 260).

OUTCOME III:

Each successful wave of the false fringe of the charismatic movement has claimed that revival is "just around the corner."

With rising disenchantment, Gerald has decided to manufacture his own revival, Rodney Howard-Browne style, in the heart of the UK, Westminster, and in Wembley Stadium. Complete with Dale Gentry, the sub-Rodney double, asking for people to be in a "posture of receptivity" particularly to his demands for money which take up a substantial part of the meeting—where the preaching of the Gospel used to go in real revivals. Rodney's, "line-'em-up-and-knock-em-down" technique is enjoyed by many, as is widespread untranslated tongues ("But if there be no interpreter. let him keep silence in the church: and let him speak to himself. and to God" I Corinthians 14:28). Gerald tries his hand at a bit of Benny Hinn "blowing the anointing" but looks a bit disgruntled as he doesn't seem to have the same devastating effect as Hinn or Hinn's role model, Kathryn Kuhlman. In the absence of any message whatsoever (except that the "christian" pop group Delirious? are in the Top Ten). The only gospel that can be preached is the gospel of "revival"—that is weird ecstatic experiences and general mayhem. Revival has replaced the Lord Jesus as the key word. The whole experience is a bizarre mixture of the terrifying and the unutterably boring, which seems to me the quintessence of hell. I tried to help a girl who was attempting to drink from a bottle but could not because "God" had made her jerk and shake so alarmingly she couldn't get it to her lips. Many professing non-Christians went to the front to be zapped with the "Holy Spirit" (despite the fact they haven't repented and don't know Christ at all), and got up again absolutely none the wiser about the person of the Lord Jesus Christ—the only means of their salvation. Apart from anything else, a perfect opportunity for the true Gospel is disgustingly wasted every night (this is a six-week revival, you see). The violence of Dale Gentry as he dragged people to the floor had to be seen to be believed, as well as his quite obvious use of kundalini yoga chakra points on people's bodies (especially the "crown chakra" on the top of the head. which is said to govern spiritual receptivity and the chakras at the belly and the base of the spine). Kundalini may or may not be a genuine psychic/demonic power, but it certainly helps to push someone over if you've got a hand on their head, and the other on their back!

> And many will follow their destructive ways, because of whom the way of truth will be blasphemed. By covetousness they will exploit you with deceptive words (2 Peter 2:2-3).

Gerald, like Nicky Gumbel, does not acknowledge that there is false teaching in the church, only "Pharisaism" from those who are earnest to discern "the spirit of truth and the spirit of error" (I John 4:6). The Pharisees were never interested in the Truth. They didn't even recognise Him when He was talking to them! In fact their preoccupation with having a large group of followers was their downfall! "If we let him thus alone, all men will believe on him: and the Romans shall come and take away both our place and nation" (John 11:48). The big-shot cult personalities have hijacked the term "Pharisee" and have misapplied it to all those who dare to question their ministries. But the truth of the matter is that their fixation with empire-building and earthly recognition is far more Pharisaical than those they threaten.

WE END WITH A few quotes from Gerald that both he and we

would do well to put into practice:

• "We create a high trust factor . . . [by] honouring our words and promises" (*The Vision*, 128.)
• "The Apostle Paul made it clear that even the prophetic church will only 'know' in part" (Ibid., 154).
• "Some of the things I said, both privately and publicly, were what I wanted to believe had happened. Accountability was needed" (!!! *An Intelligent Fire*, 81).
• He also says in a couple of places how he rejects untranslated tongues (never mind the fact that the "Sowing the Seeds of Revival" videos start with several minutes of it).
• He resents speakers with their "thus sayeth the Lord" approach. Dale Gentry, however, is entirely backed by Coates as he proclaims that "the Holy Spirit spoke to me last Thursday and said, 'There's a revival in Westminster.'" That is to say, we've given up waiting and hyping so let's just pretend it's here and if we shout loudly enough. maybe the people will believe us.

As Gerald quotes at the beginning of his chapter, "The Visionary": "Where there is no vision the people are unrestrained . . . " (Proverbs 29:13, NASB).

Let us earnestly petition the Lord that He may restore restraint, truth, vision and real blessing to a church direly in need of Biblical reform, that we might "repent and do the first works," especially in proclaiming the simple power of the Gospel of the Lord Jesus Christ!

As I write this, I feel increasingly burdened that we respond to the issues raised and the people concerned with discernment and compassion in equal measure. It is frighteningly easy to fall into either the camp of "it's all over, the global deception is here" heresy hunters, or the "welcome the new dawn of world revival" charismaniacs. The Truth Himself promised His Spirit, and that He would "guide us into all truth" (John 16: 13). We must work so, so hard at learning how to speak that truth in love, so that all sincere believers "may grow up in all things into him who is the head—Christ" (Ephesians 4:15). We all have a lot of growing up to do: some of us need to consider "whether we want to win [people over] or simply point out their error" (Coates, *The Vision*); others of us may want to think about whether we care about truth at all. We all need the Lord's tremendous grace that we might daily demonstrate that "love which covers over a multitude of sins" (Proverbs 10: 12, I Peter 4:8).

For those (like me!) prone to seeing leaven in every lump, check out the admonition to the Ephesian church in Revelation 2. For others who tend to see more with rose-tinted specs than with the eyes of discernment, don't miss the message to the church in Pergamum in the same chapter (especially verse 15).

One final comment: if you come away from reading this concerned about Gerald Coates, put it into action in praying for him and those whom he influences. If you come away feeling offended or outraged, please pray for me!

> Let the words of my mouth and the meditation of my heart be acceptable in your sight, O LORD, my strength and redeemer (Psalm 19: 14).

Endnotes

Introduction

1 http://www.streamsministries.com/news/2013-08-01/unlocking-the-dream-code-john-paul-jackson-explains-8-dream-symbols
2 Todd Bentley, "Prophetic Word for 2008," www.elijahlist.com
3 "Ekstasis Worship-What is it?," *Elijah List*, August 11 ,2008, http://www.elijahlist.com/words/display_word/6737)
4 Ibid.

Chapter 1

1 Prophecy published by the Sweetwater Church of the Valley, Pastor Glenn Foster, *Life for the Nations*, October 7, 1994
2 Advertisement for "Seers Convocation," *Charisma* Magazine, date unknown
3 Discernment Research Group, http://herescope.blogspot.com/2007/03/return-of-warrior-prophets.html
4 Bill Hamon, *Prophets and Personal Prophecy*, Destiny Image Publishers; 10th printing edition, July 1, 1987, pg. 28
5 H. A. Ironside, H. A. *The Mission of the Holy Spirit*, Kindle Locations 526-532, CrossReach Publications. Kindle Edition.

Chapter 2

1 Ern Baxter, National Men's Shepherds Conference, Kansas City, Missouri, Sept. 1975
2 Earl Paulk, *The Wounded Body of Christ*, as quoted in Jewel van der Merwe's book *Joel's Army*
3 William W. Menzies, *Anointed to Serve, The Story of the Assemblies of God*, Gospel Publishing House, Springfield Mo., 1971, pg. 32
4 J. Preston Eby, *The Battle of Armageddon, Part IV*, Kingdom Bible Studies, September 1976, pg. 10; quoted in Richard Michael Riss, *The Latter Rain Movement of 1948 and the Mid-Twentieth Century Evangelical Awakening*, April 1979, pg. 197
5 Bill Hamon, *Prophets and the Prophetic Movement*, Destiny Image Publishers, October 1, 1990

6   Earl Paulk, *The Wounded Body of Christ*, Dimension Publishers,2nd edition, 1985

Chapter 3
1   William Branham, *Footprints on the Sands of Time*, MacMillian, Reprint edition, 1983, pg. 94
2   Gordon Lindsay, *William Branham, A Man Sent From God*, Introduction
3   From Branham's message, "How the Gift Came To Me," preached April 1948
4   Lindsay, pg. 77
5   Vinson Synan, *Voices of Pentecost: Testimonies of Lives Touched by the Holy Spirit*, Vibe Books, 2003, pg. 28
6   William Branham, "Adoption," Voice of God Recordings, 1977
7   Kurt Koch, *Between Christ and Satan*, Kregel, 1962
8   Ibid.
9   Al Dager, *Vengeance is Ours*, Sword Publishing, 1990)
10 http://www.letusreason.org/Latrain3.htm

Chapter 4
1   http://www.bobjones.org/Docs/Prophetic%20Archives/1999_Remnant_Seed.htm, accessed July 17, 2015
2   Bill Hamon, *Prophets and Personal Prophecy, God's Prophetic Voice Today*, Destiny Image Press, 1987, pg. 53
3   "The Prophetic History of Grace Ministries," Kansas City, Mo., Grace Ministries, n.d., cassette tape.
4   Bob Jones, "Visions and Revelations," 1988, cassette tape
5   Ibid.
6   Mike Bickle, spoken at Anaheim Vineyard 1989, http://www.discernment-ministries.com/Newsletters/NL1990Aug.pdf, accessed July 17, 2015
7   Mike Bickle, Bob Jones, "The Shepherd's Rod.," Fall, 1989, audio recording
8   Al Dager, *Vengeance is Ours*, Sword Publishing 1990)
9   Mike Bickle, Michael Sullivant, "God's Manifest Presence: Understanding the Phenomena that Accompany the Spirit's Ministry," Metro Vineyard Fellowship, 1995
10 Paul Cain, taped message
11 Vineyard Prophecy School, 1989
12 March 8, 1998, Crossroads, Hamilton, Ontario

Chapter 5

1   Rick Joyner, *The Harvest: The Prophetic Word of the Nineties and Beyond*, Morningstar Publications, 1989
2   Ibid, pg. 74, 75
3   Ibid.
4   Ibid.
5   Ibid.
6   Rick Joyner, Harvest Conference, Denver, November, 1990
7   Rick Joyner, *The Final Quest*, Morningstar Publications, 2006, pg. 37
8   Ibid.
9   Ibid.
10 Kevin Reeves, "Those Who Resist," http://www.lighthousetrailsresearch.com/blog/?p=1792, accessed July 20, 2015

Chapter 6

1   Bill Randles, *Weighed and Found Wanting*, Dick Sleeper Distribution, 1996
2   Ibid., pg. 59, 60
3   Pam Sollner, *The Olathe Daily News*, Nov. 13, 1991
4   *Charisma News*, February 2005
5   http://mikebickle.org/resources/series/38 accessed 7/22/2015
6   http://unsettledchristianity.com/2009/12/say-about-mike-bickle-and-the-ihop-cult-i-wasnt-kidding/
7   http://gospelmasquerade.wordpress.com/2009/02/18/why-i-believe-ihop-is-a-cult/
8   Keith Gibson, 2007, http://beyondgrace.blogspot.com/2012/11/ihop-sensual-teaching-and-pratices-led.html, accessed July 22, 2015
9   http://www.seekalyric.com/song/John_Mark_Mcmillan/How_He_Loves
10 http://www.hishousemedia.com/docs/BreakingNews.htm, accessed July 22, 2015
11 Ibid.
12 http://mywordlikefire.com/2011/07/29/mike-bickle-of-ihop-wants-book-about-catholic-mystics-to-be-manual-for-ihop-kc/, accessed July 22, 2015
13 http://mikebickle.org/resources/resource/1529?return_url=http%3A%2F%2Fmikebickle.org%2Fresources%2Fcategory%2Fministry-outreach%2Fprophetic-ministry%2F, accessed July 22, 2015

14 http://mywordlikefire.com/2011/10/28/mike-bickle-of-ihop-kc-instructs-followers-on-contemplative-prayer/, accessed July 22, 2015
15 http://mikebickle.org/resources/resource/1529?return_url=http%3A%2F%2Fmikebickle.org%2Fresources%2Fcategory%2Fministry-outreach%2Fprophetic-ministry%2F
16 Mike Bickle, "Contemplative Prayer Part 1," audio recording

Chapter 7

1 http://www.irishcentral.com/news/us-based-preacher-who-heals-by-punching-and-kicking-banned-from-northern-ireland-video-167304455-237524741.html#ixzz2vhaExm9z
2 "Leaders Commission Todd Bentley at Lakeland Outpouring," *Charisma*, June 24, 2008
3 Ibid.
4 Ibid.
5 Ibid.
6 Ibid.
7 A. J. Appasamy, *Sundar Singh*, Lutterwork Press, 2003, pg. 68
8 http://web.archive.org/web/20080501145425/http://www.freshfire.ca/teaching_details.php?Id=143, accessed July 22, 2015
9 https://sheepyweepy.wordpress.com/category/east-meets-west/

Chapter 8

1 *The Supernatural Power of a Transformed Mind*, Destiny Image Publishers, first edition, January 1, 2005, pg. 50
2 Bill Johnson, *Face to Face with God,* 2007, Charisma House, Lake Mary, FL., pg. 200
3 Bill Johnson, *When Heaven Invades Earth*, Destiny Image Publishers, 2005, pg. 87
4 Ibid.
5 http://beyondgrace.blogspot.com/2011/07/bill-johnson-and-john-crowders-leaven.html;   http://www.youtube.com/watch?v=L-rHPTs8cLls https://www.facebook.com/photo.
6 http://gospelliving.blogspot.com/2013/04/why-jesus-culture-bethel-church-and_15.html
7 Johnson, *When Heaven Invades Earth, pg.* 93)

Chapter 9

1 Advertisement for C Peter Wagner's National School of the Prophets Conference, January 1999

2 Hamon, *Prophets and Personal Prophecy*
3 Ibid.
4 Bill Hamon, *The Eternal Church*, Destiny Image Publishers, January 1, 2005. pg. 333
5 http://marcdupontministries.com/about/
6 Ibid.
7 Marc DuPont, "Lion of Judah," cassette message
8 Ibid.
9 Marc DuPont, Prophetic School, 1994).
10 Ibid.
11 James Ryle, "Sons of Thunder," Harvest Conference, Denver Colorado, November, 1990

Chapter 10
1 John Arnott, Toronto Airport Vineyard, December, 1994

Chapter 11
1 Hamon, *Prophets and Personal Prophecy*
2 Stephen Strang, "A Caution On Personal Prophecy," *Charisma Magazine*, September 1989
3 Rick Joyner, "The Prophetic Ministry," *Morningstar Prophetic Newsletter,*Vol. 3, No. 2, pg. 2
4 Ibid.
5 David Pytches, *Some Said It Thundered*, Thomas Nelson Inc., March 1991, pg. 108-109
6 C. Douglas Weaver, *The Healer Prophet*, Mercer University Press, November 1, 2000
7 Al Dager, "Latter Day Prophets," Media Spotlight Special Report
8 Hamon, *Prophets and Personal Prophecy*
9 Mike Bickle, *Growing in the Prophetic*, Charisma House, Revised edition, November 4, 2008

Chapter 12
1 Judy Franklin and Ellyn Davis, *The Physics of Heaven*, Destiny Image Publishers, 2012
2 Ibid.
3 Ibid.
4 Benny Hinn sermon, "Double Portion Anointing, Part #3," Orlando Christian Center, Orlando, Fla., April 7, 1991. From the series, "Holy Ghost Invasion," TV#309, tape on file

5   "Welcome back Midaeival Catholicism, prayers to the dead, relics and Holy Places," Bethel Students "Soaking Anointing" Off of Tombs, http://beyondgrace.blogspot.com/2011/07/bill-johnson-and-john-crowders-leaven.html
6   Judy Franklin and Ellyn Davis, *The Physics of Heaven*

Chapter 13
1   John Wimber, "Unpacking Your Bags," audio tape, date unknown

Chapter 14
1   Paul Cain and Rick Joyner, "The Clinton Administration Its Meaning and Our Future," *Morningstar Prophetic Bulletin #3*, January, 1993
2   Irenaeus, *Against Heresies*, Preface 2, c180-190 AD)
3   Paul Cain and Rick Joyner, "The Clinton Administration Its Meaning and Our Future"
4   Jewel van der Merwe, "Prophets, Etc.," *Discernment,* March/April, 1993
5   Ibid.

Chapter 15
1   https://renewaljournal.wordpress.com/2011/07/18/the-power-to-heal-the-past-by-c-peter-wagner/
2   C. Peter Wagner, *Engaging the Enemy*, Regal Books, pg. 46
3   John Goodwin, "Testing the Fruit of the Vineyard," *Media Spotlight Report*

Appendix 2
1   "Laughing for the Lord," *Time* Magazine, August 15, 1994
2   From the Fathers Day video, June, 1995
3   Nicholas Monson, "Congregation Rolling in the Aisle," *Sunday Telegraph*, Sunday 19th June 1994.

Other Books
by Pastor Bill Randles

Making War in the Heavenlies: A different look at Spiritual Warfare- (1994) Pastor Bill was asked in 1994 to explain why he wasn't leading his church into various aspects of city wide spiritual warfare exercising, such as prayer walking, March for Jesus, naming the demons over the city, binding and loosing ,etc. Out of that explanation came this book, which discusses not only the heretical practices listed above, bit the true biblical teaching on spiritual warfare.

Weighed and Found Wanting: Putting the Toronto Blessing in Context- (1995)- Thousands of Christians were traveling to the Toronto Airport Vineyard to experience "a new anointing," and Spiritual Drunkenness. Was this really "as a rushing mighty wind from heaven" as its proponents claimed? Pastor Bill refutes this notion, having traced the "revival" back to its roots in the Manifested Sons of God heresy, once rebuked and rejected by the Assemblies of God, but now widely accepted as a mighty revival.

Born From Above: An Exposition of John Chapter 3 (2015) - This is an exposition of the third chapter of the Gospel of John, one of the most familiar and beloved chapters in the New Testament. In this brief study,Pastor Bill shows the continuity of the theme, the New Birth as taught by Jesus, in a conversation with one of the greatest and most renown theologians of his day, Nicodemus. Pastor Bill Sheds new light on familiar texts such as John 3:16. This book is expositional and evangelistic as well. It would be great for Bible Studies.

Mending The Nets: Themes and Commentary of First John - In this book Pastor Bill explores the undergirding themes of first John, such as eternal life, the tests of eternal life, true and false faith, the Gnostic redefinition of the knowledge of God, and the true knowledge of God. Like John, Pastor Bill takes us back to the beginning, the first thing revealed in the gospel of Jesus . This commentary is relevant to the current apostasy in the church.

A Sword On The Land: The Muslim World in Bible Prophecy - (2013) The 2011 "Arab Spring" was significant, but not for the reasons the world hoped for. Pastor Bill, in a very readable style, explains that rather than being a movement towards democracy in the Arab world, the real significance was the setting in place of the nations of the Middle East for the fulfillment of endgames prophecies.

CPSIA information can be obtained
at www.ICGtesting.com
Printed in the USA
LVOW08s1609160817
545245LV00015B/1476/P